The Greatest of These

A Memoir

Lori Morrison

The Greatest of These
Copyright © 2019 Lori Morrison
All rights reserved.

Cover by Brienne Sambell
Formatting by Polgarus Studio

ISBN: 978-1-9992501-0-2
ISBN: 978-1-9992501-1-9 (ebook)

Disclaimer: This memoir is a truthful recollection of actual events in the author's life. Conversations and events have been recreated from memory, journal entries and letters. Some names and identifying details have been changed or left out to protect the privacy of individuals.

Contents

Seems you paid too high a price
And fell so very far
To be taken to the depths
and refined by the fire,
To the core of who you were
And the man that we all loved;
You've run your race with a rebel yell,
A lion heart and a gentle soul;
A man whose smile and laugh
Was as blazing as the sun;
A friend to the forgotten,
A father oh so proud,
And a husband reconciled;
A man whose loving spirit
Has finally been set free
To shimmer on the water
Or mingle with the clouds;
Forever intertwined
With the ones you've left behind

Preface

For as long as I can remember, the idea of being a writer appealed to me, like a buried treasure that somehow seemed possible to find. However, in the life I found myself living, the struggles and the chaos took precedence and it looked as though there was no way for that dream to ever come true. When I reached a point in my life where I came to the end of my self sufficiency, where I felt completely powerless and with no idea what to do, I surrendered to God. I couldn't have imagined what I was in for. Taken on an incredibly dark journey of long-suffering, I watched God work miracles in the midst of tragedy.

During that time, through my work, I was in contact with a Postmaster who was also a published author of poetry. Unsatisfied with my effort to write about my life and the trauma I was living at the time, Anders Carson sparked the inspiration to try writing poetry. His praise and encouragement spurred me on to write a small book of poetry. The poems became a means of catharsis but also a way to infuse life into my writing when all I felt around me was death.

After my husband passed away, on the very last day of 2017, I prayed for God to show me a new purpose. When I decided to attend a new church near my home, it was the first Easter Sunday service. After the service, a woman who was there with her daughter introduced herself. In speaking with her, I discovered that her young daughter was a type I diabetic. This struck me as significant because my husband had been a type I diabetic from the age of twelve. Later in the conversation, the woman told me about a Christian writer's conference coming up in Michigan and she was encouraging me to go. She also said that she was supposed to meet me. I never saw her again at that church.

The excitement that I felt, believing that this was God's direction, broke through the lethargy borne out of my mourning and drove me to tell my story.

Chapter One
Runaway Train

You weren't willing to give or willing to see
And you watched me crumble as I ran
To pick up the pieces of you and of me
As they blew off the wreck that flew down the tracks

Stepping on the accelerator to take us onto the highway, my heart started to race and I tried to catch my breath. I may as well have had my foot pushing down on a pedal labelled "panic." It was January 2013, and I was driving my husband to the nearest metropolis for step one in a series of tests and meetings required for him to undergo another pancreas transplant. Crashing the car seemed entirely possible so, in an attempt to calm myself down, I started to breathe like they tell you when you're in labour. My husband was a bit concerned but certainly not as much as he should have been. All I wanted to do was get out of that car, shut down the mental image of the fiery ball of wreckage and have my feet touch the ground. Later I thought to myself—*that must be what it feels like to have a panic attack.*

At the time I didn't really understand why, but there was a sickening momentum like I was being held hostage on a runaway train. Ever since my husband, Leigh, decided he wanted to go ahead with the transplant, uneasiness took hold of me and wouldn't let go. I tried to ignore the dread because I couldn't grasp anything with confidence and say, "Hey, it's just not a good idea." Leigh had good reason to want the transplant. He was so determined to push ahead, not even a herd of wild horses could hold him back. His driver's license had been taken away from him after his last diabetic seizure, and, in his mind's eye, the transplant was the ticket to regaining his freedom.

Leigh had undergone a double kidney-pancreas transplant in 2009, and the way I felt back then was completely different. Sure, I had fear, but it felt like we were all in it together—my husband, myself and our young daughter—waiting for a miracle. Leigh was only in his forties when he lost all kidney function. He had to have a tube implanted into his abdomen so he could be hooked up to a dialysis machine for ten hours a day. We wanted him to have a working kidney, to be free from the dialysis machine and everything that went with it. We wanted him to be able to go on bike rides with us and not feel weak or faint. We wanted him to have a working pancreas so he could leave behind all the worries that came with the diabetes he had had since childhood. That was the collective want. The part that I wanted for myself was to be released from the constant worry over his diabetic seizures. I always had to be "on"—like my stress hormones were in a permanent standby position. Leigh's seizures could happen any time: in the middle of the night, out in public, at work or even while driving. In fact, at times I found myself resentful because Leigh didn't appear to worry about it that much. When one of them hit, he was completely out of it and I was pretty much always the one who had to take care of it. On one hand, you could admire how he never let his diabetes stop him from trying to live a normal life. On the other hand, I used the catch phrase "denial ain't just a river in Egypt" to describe my husband's strategy for dealing with the parts of his life he didn't want to deal with.

Leigh became a type I diabetic at the age of twelve, and he required multiple injections of insulin every day. Despite what many people may think, insulin is not a cure and not all diabetes can be well managed. Leigh had a particularly severe, difficult-to-control form of the disease called brittle diabetes. He had experienced countless seizures and even a coma before I ever knew him. My life prior to Leigh was full of rejection and abuse, so the fact that he seemed to need me was like the drug I didn't know I craved. As my husband's problems and needs became the main focus of our lives, these things took over my identity. My worth had become completely wrapped up in looking after him, looking after our daughter and keeping our family afloat financially.

My husband had a good heart and that's why I fell in love with him; he had a genuine warmth and an easy going way about him that people were drawn to. He would often say of himself that he loves everybody. However admirable these qualities might be, he had a lack of discernment regarding people and was easily taken advantage of. He would back away from conflict, especially in those instances where he should have taken a stand. This part of his disposition became a major problem for me, and, as a result, our marriage started to suffer.

Dialysis was very hard on him; the treatments were time-consuming and restricting. They tired him out, and he was susceptible to infections. At the same time, he was trying to manage his diabetes and keep working in a physical job. He would never say it but I knew he was hurting because his family wasn't there for him; they tended to minimize what was happening and the prevailing attitude was that dialysis wasn't a big deal.

The circumstances surrounding their attitude was complicated and I certainly didn't have all of it figured out back then. There had been a coldness filling in the space between us and Leigh's family in the years leading up to Leigh's kidney failure. And, along with everything we were facing, the hostility that was coming our way was as puzzling as it was unbearable.

We had just come back from a vacation, and I was feeling positive, even though we were adjusting to the reality that things were going to be rough with Leigh going on dialysis soon. It was an active trip; we were taking our daughter, Brienne, to meet her friend who was camping in Northern Ontario. On the way, we were canoeing in Algonquin Park—the kind of trip Leigh wouldn't be able to take again for the foreseeable future.

Something happened when we came back home that, on the surface, seemed trivial. Even though there were many things I wasn't yet aware of, I knew immediately after it happened that it was indicative of the silent storm that had been brewing, and it was pivotal.

Leigh's father Willie called. He demanded to know when Leigh could help him move a chimney on an old house he had just bought. Over the years, I had become unsettled by my father-in-law's behaviour and avoided picking up his calls. For a long time, I accepted the general consensus that he was eccentric but, gradually, intuition told me that something wasn't quite right with him. He was completely oblivious and unconcerned with his son's health challenges and how they affected him personally or how they affected his ability to make a living and help support us. These, of course, became my burdens, which seemed to concern Willie even less.

Normally, I would have let his call go to voice mail, but this time I asked Brienne to pick it up. Leigh was asleep; he was working on an on-call basis with a new employer and had to be ready to take a shift at any time. Even though our daughter told him that his son was asleep, he insisted on talking to me instead and proceeded to grill me on when Leigh would be available to help him. Offering to have Leigh call him back when he woke up was not enough. He was like a dog with a bone; he wouldn't let it go. The nitty-gritty was that he wanted a commitment that Leigh was going to be able to do what he wanted, when he wanted it done. My voice was shaking with anger. When he objected to my tone, I blurted out, "You push and you push and you push, that's why." I said good-bye and hung up.

Being defiant, however minor, to a man who was used to having his own way was completely out of character for me. I certainly wasn't raised to have any confidence in myself. Little did I know that the road ahead would force me to stand my ground and push back over and over again.

The dominoes started to fall as Leigh's mother, Hattie, called about five minutes later with words full of vitriol. She said I was rude and had always been rude to them. Being in shock through the entire scolding left my memory numbed to all that was said. It wasn't fair and it wasn't true, but there was a part of me—the little girl who had been shamed by her mother—that believed it nonetheless.

When I met Leigh, I started to spend a lot of time with his family because they appeared to be like the normal, loving family I never had. Years of my life were invested in trying to fit in to this family but Hattie's verbal attack seemed to be proof that it was all for nothing. How could she not see that all I was doing was protecting her son, my husband?

After that, I told Leigh that I was done trying to please his family, offering to divorce him if that would make things easier. He didn't want that, but in pressing him to stand up for himself or for me, he would sidestep the issue. Leigh's default position was to have his head firmly buried in the sand but it would have been hard to miss that I was more than a little upset. A week or two passed before he made an attempt to discuss the matter with his father. Then, when he did, I was disappointed with how eager he was to accept Willie's excuse. Willie took no responsibility and attributed the verbal attack on me to all the prescription drugs that his wife was taking. At the time I was too distraught to make a lot of sense of what had happened.

On another occasion, when Leigh tried to meet with both of his parents to discuss what happened with me, they didn't show up. Even though I was angry and hurt, I realized that Leigh's mother was in a difficult position. She depended on Willie, such as he was. When I was dating Leigh, we'd shared conversations in which she admitted that there had been serious trouble in her marriage—serious enough for her to want to leave. She stayed because she was afraid of him and didn't know how she would support herself and three young children.

So, for the years Leigh was on dialysis there was little to no communication between me and Leigh's family. Leigh missed having them in his life, and he wanted to carry on like nothing ever happened. Part of me wanted to go along, for his sake and for my daughter's sake, but I just couldn't bring myself to do it—to walk into their lives again and pretend it was okay. My feelings didn't appear to matter so I did my best to accept that my husband and daughter would go see his family at Christmas and on other occasions. I wasn't part of it anymore, and they seemed content with that. Willie was lining up the family against me—using my hurt and my silence as leverage to do so. I heard that he was telling Leigh and his brother, Peter, that I was crazy like my mentally ill mother.

His strategy for getting to me was working because the atmosphere of antipathy was inescapable, even when I wanted to turn to my own husband for understanding. But then I discovered that there was a psychological term for what he was doing; he was gas lighting me. There was more to it than a garden-variety cruelty. It was a manipulation designed to isolate me, to question my perceptions and even my own sanity. Despite the relief in finally realizing that this was a lie, it felt like I was being buried alive with no choice but to be silent because no one else could see it.

My husband was trying to work as much as he could and hooking himself up to the dialysis machine every night like a sci-fi cyborg. For my part, I was determined to help him and keep our little family going. The core problems between Leigh and me were still there, but his need for my support brought out more humility and more appreciation.

I believed that Leigh loved me but, at the same time, he seemed unable to show it in any way that mattered to me. Maybe I was awakening to a realization that I had accepted too little for too long. If I brought up how much I had done for him, he would acknowledge it but it didn't change how he behaved. Over time his words meant less and less because it became painfully obvious that I was not a priority. For instance, there was the time that Leigh was supposed to meet me at the auto repair shop, so I didn't have to wait while my car was being looked after. But he forgot because his father had called him for something, so he dropped everything to go see him. Of course, I was angry. But instead of acknowledging the validity of why I was angry, the next day when I was at work, Leigh called me and started talking about suicide.

He was saying how he couldn't handle being on dialysis anymore and even though part of me knew this had something to do with our argument, I couldn't take a chance that he wasn't bluffing. When Leigh went on kidney dialysis, we were given access to a social worker, a dietician and other healthcare professionals to help in the transition. I begged someone to cover for me at work while I arranged for the social worker to see us right away. Leigh talked about the dialysis being too difficult. Sitting there, embarrassed, I almost didn't say anything but then I told the social worker about what happened and why I was angry. After he heard both our stories, I was shocked that he reprimanded Leigh for using the threat to punish me for being angry. I wasn't used to anyone seeing or caring about my perspective.

Leigh stubbornly kept the blinders on when it came to his father, which meant he couldn't acknowledge my suffering. Therefore, my bitterness grew along with the distance between us. Whenever I did try to express myself to my husband, he took the path of least resistance: he would blame me. By nature, Leigh was easygoing, but he was reaching a point where he couldn't deny his emotions. His anger was becoming more evident, especially after he lost his driver's license. It's no exaggeration to say that, at times, I was afraid of him.

He claimed to want to fix things between us so I suggested counselling. However, I didn't go into it with high expectations because I knew Leigh wasn't hearing me. I didn't trust him anymore and I didn't know how to fix that by myself. There were too many times that he didn't put me first, that he wasn't there for me, that he wouldn't defend me. These were the things I wanted to discuss with the counsellor but he deflected and tried to make it about something else. When I brought up his family and how he put them first, he said that was because he had known them longer. He didn't even realize that he had dug the hole even deeper, strengthening my case.

Whenever I thought about ending the relationship, I always came back to the idea that I needed to be there in case something happened. I knew, in going through the kidney failure and dialysis experience with him, that there wouldn't be anyone else to give him the help he needed if anything went wrong. It always came back to that—that he needed me. How had it come to this? Why should I be so compelled to act as his saviour? It wasn't just him, though. What about our daughter? What about the finances? He wouldn't be able to manage living on his own; he could have a seizure alone somewhere and end up dead. I wanted out, but I couldn't live with the idea of abandoning him. I didn't know who I was, having invested almost twenty years into this marriage. Had I been wrong in trying to do the right thing by sticking it out in a relationship that I am certain many women would have bailed on a long time ago?

There was no balance. I had been doing all the giving and I didn't have anything left. *This was my crisis point.*

As far back as I can remember, I sensed that there was more to the world than could be seen. I believed in God and it bothered me that Leigh didn't. I admit that I was ignorant about what that meant for me or my life, and I can't say that I knew anything about the experience of a personal relationship with God. I kept trying my best to have a normal life, be a good person, and live my life striving after what I wanted—the way the rest of the world does. Why am I saying this? Because, it was leading up to this transplant that I finally hit an emotional rock bottom that brought me to my knees. I had gone through some pretty horrible things, aside from what I had dealt with in my marriage to Leigh. But I suffered and pushed through as best I could, praying here and there, believing that someday all my striving would be rewarded. This time, I was literally on the floor of my closet, my soul in pure anguish, crying out to God. How could this be where my best efforts ended up? Waves of regret washed over me as I begged God to forgive my mistakes and restore all that had been stolen from me. People had treated me badly throughout my life, I had sacrificed myself in a marriage where I felt like a chained ghost, believing that I had let God down by not fulfilling His purpose for me. Furthermore, I still didn't know what that purpose was. Now, there I was, trying to be supportive for my husband, who was facing a major surgery, but my heart wasn't in it. I still loved Leigh as a person, but, not the way you should in a marriage. I felt completely alone.

After that first trip to the big city, I knew I couldn't handle it. The thought of driving there and having another panic attack filled me with such dread that I decided we would take the train or I would send Leigh on his own. It was a risk letting him go alone but stepping back a bit was the only way I could cope. After Leigh had gone on his own once or twice, the transplant coordinator called and begged me to come with him. One of the other big challenges with Leigh was his inability to accurately communicate. Often, he would completely misconstrue or forget things altogether. I know that a lot of men have poor communication skills, but Leigh took it to a whole other level, and I attributed it to the fact that he was dyslexic. When you asked him about something someone had said or about something important, you never really knew if what you were hearing was true, half true, or completely wrong. When the transplant coordinator expressed her frustration, I said "Welcome to my world."

I remember the appointment we both attended with the Director of Surgery. He wanted us to be aware of the risk, but he appeared quite confident overall. He painted a picture of how good this would be—how freeing it would be. The main danger seemed to be organ rejection, particularly with the pancreas. Yes, the pancreas was a tricky little organ.

Leigh and I discussed the risk, but he was determined to go ahead so I put aside my apprehension to support him. That vision—the one where he could drive again and didn't have to take needles or bother with the insulin pump—obscured any flicker of caution that may have danced across his mind.

The call finally came on the morning of August 1, 2013. Leigh called me at work and said we had to leave for the big city. My anxiety was starting to build again and I could feel my heart beating faster. We quickly packed and were on our way when we received another call saying that it was going to be delayed until the next morning. We decided to continue onward and stay the night so that we could be at the hospital first thing in the morning.

We arrived very early the next morning and I remember thinking how strange it was: it was almost eerie, like a twilight zone. There wasn't anyone around, and this was a very large city hospital. We reached the empty registration desk. When a man arrived, and we explained that Leigh was there for his transplant, he wasn't in a great hurry to usher us in. Again, it was strange—this wasn't exactly toenail surgery.

We were left sitting in an empty hallway for what seemed like forever. Then our daughter called us from our home, a two hour drive away. She had received a call from the hospital, the very one we were sitting in, and the transplant unit was wondering where we were! Half jokingly, I said to my husband, "Should we be going ahead with this? This is so ridiculous! We announced that we're here for your transplant, then we're left sitting in a hallway and now they don't know where we are. Apparently, the left hand doesn't know what the right hand is doing." This was just another one of those moments where I pushed aside that little niggling sense that something didn't feel right. Even though I believed in God, I didn't recognize the sense as being His voice at the time. Other forces were at work, making it seem like the only logical choice. Leigh desperately wanted the surgery, the medical professionals were confident, all the tests gave the green light and we were there now with a pancreas and surgeons ready to go.

It took almost seven hours for a team of surgeons to weave their human tapestry—a delicate fusion of life and death. Someone we didn't know had died to give Leigh this gift, and the enormity of it was humbling. I was alone, waiting in a sort of time-suspension torture because it just didn't feel right. The cell phone woke me out of a surface sleep; it was one of the surgeons calling to say all had gone well.

When I saw Leigh the next morning, my uneasiness appeared to be completely unfounded. He was in good spirits and he was alert. I stayed in the city for a few days to make sure he was okay before going home to be with Brienne. It was my understanding that Leigh would be in hospital for a couple of weeks, and, after that, he would have to stay somewhere close by for another week or two for follow-ups. My plan was to wait for the call that he was being released from hospital before making the trip back.

At the end of the first week, Leigh phoned home to say that he was being released. I reminded him of what we had been told about him having to stay in the city for follow-ups. He insisted that he was told by one of the doctors assigned to his case that he could go home, and the transplant hospital there could do the assessments. I was shocked and skeptical. Looking back, I should have known better. I probably should have insisted on talking to one of the doctors myself, but because he seemed so certain, Brienne and I made the trip to bring him home.

We arrived and found Leigh waiting for us in the Transplant Unit on the sixth floor. I asked him if he had everything he needed; he said he did, and it was evident he couldn't wait to leave. So, we informed the staff on that floor that we were leaving, and there was no objection. Tired and overwhelmed, I didn't get into questioning him the way I normally would. Another part of it was my own lack of desire or will to continue micromanaging every detail of Leigh's life.

The three of us made our way down to the main floor, and as we were getting off the elevator we ran into the pharmacist. She was surprised when I told her that Leigh had been discharged. She said there was a process for release that involved Leigh checking in with the pharmacy regarding his medications and meeting with someone about care and follow-up appointments. Leigh appeared to be unaware of any of this. At that point, my stress level shot through the roof as I realized Leigh had screwed this up. He had not taken care of all of this before we got there, and it was all I could do to focus and maintain some composure. I was left to try and sort out where we should go and what exactly needed to be done. We went back upstairs to the pharmacy and to a meeting about Leigh's follow-up appointments, which we would need to come back for. Finally, when we were finished with all that, we took a cab to the train station and headed back home.

I was starting to feel more relaxed as the train got closer to the station where I had parked the car. As we were pulling into the station, my cell phone rang. It was the Surgical Director, the head surgeon that we had met with prior to the transplant. He was angry and wanted to know why we had left the hospital! I was completely taken off guard, and I couldn't believe what I was hearing. Of course I responded with what Leigh had told me. He accused me of risking my husband's life by taking him out of hospital. So, here we were in the train station, taking turns on the cell phone being lectured and reprimanded by the surgeon. He ended up saying that we better get our butts back to the hospital. You could have knocked me over with a feather at that point. I was at my wits end, and I was embarrassed, angry and exhausted.

We bought our tickets and got back on the train. It was getting late and I didn't know where we were going to go once we arrived. I called the hospital and spoke to at least two people, explaining the situation, but they refused to re-admit him! Their explanation was that we should have prearranged accommodation. I had actually booked Leigh into a residence-type hotel starting the next week, when I had expected him to be discharged. Therefore, looking back, I'm certain he was discharged when he shouldn't have been. I was furious. Several of the staff knew we were leaving, and no one told us otherwise. Now that he was supposed to go back, they wouldn't let him in the door.

Brienne and I only had the clothes we were wearing, and Leigh didn't have much with him either. I booked us in at a hotel that was near the downtown train station. We tried to sleep, but Leigh and I were both too upset to get much rest. I kept rehearsing what I was going to say to the transplant coordinator when I saw her. It was the weekend and Leigh's first follow-up appointment wasn't until mid-week. What a complete fiasco. I couldn't believe it; but, then again, I could—that is how my life with Leigh always was. This was only another lightning strike in the chaos that Leigh attracted.

We needed to bide our time until I could get us checked in at the next hotel, so we went out for breakfast and took a cab to the mall. It was apparent that Leigh shouldn't really be out anywhere; he was in a lot of pain and could barely walk. We left him on some benches while Brienne and I bought some pyjamas and supplies at the drug store, but we hadn't been gone long when he called and said he couldn't wait anymore, that he had to lie down.

Leigh had no patience for me figuring out where we should go, so we left through the nearest exit we could find. As I stood there, trying to get my bearings, Leigh kept walking right out into the intersection, paying no attention to traffic. He was narrowly missed by a taxi as we went chasing after him, yelling at him to stop. I begged him to sit down on a bench and take his medication. It wasn't a simple matter of taking something for pain. He had a laundry list of post-transplant medications, including immunosuppressant drugs that he was supposed to be taking at specific times. I walked down the block to find a taxi that would take us to the next hotel and I was relieved when they allowed us to check in early. After getting Leigh settled, Brienne and I ventured out to get some groceries to stock the kitchenette.

Finally, the day came for the follow-up appointment, and I was ready to give someone an earful about what we had been put through. However, it seemed that the transplant coordinator must have been aware of what went on. She immediately apologized and explained it away as a miscommunication for which one of the staff was reprimanded. I was still upset, but after she said that Leigh's blood work looked good and that he could go home for good, I decided I would let it go; besides, I had no energy for a fight. Oh hallelujah, happy day! The trip home was a sweet ride.

Chapter Two
Things Impending and Threatening

Triumphant fusion with the precious flesh of a stranger
Leave surgeons confident in their art
But then pride goes out the window
As death comes to the door

We were riding the wave, feeling giddy almost, as we started telling complete strangers—from the waitress at the restaurant on our first night back to the neighbour down the street as we took the dog for a walk—about our reason to celebrate.

On Leigh's second night home, he woke me up in the night; he had a high fever. We rushed to hospital with the thought that the pancreas was rejecting because we knew that fever would be a primary symptom. Days and nights went by with no answers as they struggled to keep Leigh's temperature down. All of their transplant and infectious diseases specialists couldn't come up with a reason for the fever.

The transplant team at the big city hospital was now insisting that he be cared for there rather than in the hospital at home. I thought it was all just posturing and bureaucracy. I didn't want him to go because, again, I had a feeling that this was taking us both somewhere we didn't want to go. Night was falling as I waited with my husband for the transport vehicle that would be taking him back to the big city, and the fear was visible in the tears that came to his eyes. I had never seen him cry. My friend, Joan, came with a small wooden comfort cross for Leigh, and even though he wasn't a believer, at that particular moment, he seemed genuinely grateful for it. Joan had been my friend for over two decades—the friend that God brought into my life as a reminder of His presence, before I realized how much I needed Him.

Leigh was back in the big city, and they were doing the same thing that the hospital at home had been trying to do: manage his persistent fevers with ice baths and medication while running a million tests. It was reassuring when I was finally able to talk to Leigh on the phone; no matter what was happening to him physically, he almost always had a calmness about him. Still, there were no answers, only theories. Leigh told me that one of the doctors thought it was Guillain-Barre Syndrome. After searching that on the internet, I was more freaked out than ever. I called Anna, the transplant coordinator, to try and get answers. She made it sound like Leigh had to be hallucinating because she didn't know any doctor who would be saying that. To me, that didn't make sense: I knew full well that Leigh had probably never even heard of Guillain-Barre Syndrome, so it wasn't likely that he came up with it on his own. It was more incongruity. Anna believed that Leigh was experiencing serum sickness, which is an immune system reaction to an antiserum that is given to patients following a transplant.

All of this uncertainty went on for about two weeks until the fevers finally subsided and Leigh was given the go-ahead to return home. I was on my way to get him, had parked at the train station and was boarding the train when a call came from Anna. She said that Leigh had been in the hospital cafeteria when he suddenly collapsed. The train hadn't yet left and I wasn't sure what to do; was it simply a matter of Leigh fainting because he needed more time to recuperate? Anna suggested that it wasn't that serious, so I decided to get off the train and drive home.

I drove the hour and a half to get home and had just finished preparing dinner for Brienne and me when the phone rang. It was Anna and there was an urgency in her voice this time, saying that we should come right away because Leigh was now in the Intensive Care Unit with a pulmonary embolism.

Blood clots had travelled from the veins in his legs up to his lungs. Why hadn't I continued on the train? My mind was racing and my hands and voice were shaking as I called Leigh's childhood friend, Scott. With the blessing of his wife, Kristine, Scott dropped his plans and offered to drive us. We were in his red pick up truck, racing through the dark, like slightly insane storm chasers headed towards a storm rather than away from it. One of Leigh and Scott's other friends, Andy, was on the cell, and we talked about how Leigh always came back from everything and he would do the same this time.

We arrived and Leigh was in a large room with all glass walls; I was relieved to see him conscious. He was talking to us; he was talking to one of the doctors. "Did I have a stroke?" he asked. After the doctor left, Leigh was telling us about their theories and questions. They thought he had a hole in his heart and that's why he had an irregular heart beat, but they couldn't really understand why his blood was clotting because he had been getting twice-a-day injections of the blood thinner heparin since the transplant. Nevertheless, he was doing so well that they were going to release him from the ICU and place him in an area that was highly monitored, but not as intense.

Because everything appeared to be fine, Scott decided to drive home. Brienne went with him while I stayed at a hotel. I was still on edge. Before going to sleep, I received a text from Leigh, which is something that almost never happened. He said he had eaten something, so I took that as a good sign and I was able to relax enough to fall asleep.

I was startled awake at quarter after six on the morning of September 6 by the sound of my cell phone, which was on the floor plugged into the wall. My heart leapt as I stumbled out of bed to answer it. There was a man on the other end saying that my husband had just suffered a stroke and he was being transported to a different hospital. In the confusion and terror of the moment, my brain was not really processing what was said. I had no idea where this other hospital was. Again, my impulse was to call Scott. Calmly and firmly he brought me down from my mental ledge, telling me to collect myself and get a taxi to the hospital they were taking him to.

When I arrived, the transport that was carrying my husband wasn't there yet, so I alternated pacing and sitting, checking in regularly with the lady at the Information desk. Finally, the computer indicated he had arrived, and the lady said "God Bless" as she sent me on my way to find him. The hospital was huge, and my legs were carrying me, but my brain was in a fog. Then I found the doctors who wanted to talk to me. That feeling of the surreal was upon me again, like I should be watching this on TV rather than living it. Here I was walking briskly down a long, sterile hallway behind a team of doctors, sensing the seriousness and urgency of their conversation. The main doctor, a neurologist, looked straight at me while the others stood around in a circle. She was speaking to me, but everything was out of mental focus—it was all I could do to stay standing. All I knew for sure was that this wasn't supposed to be happening.

In shock as I looked at my husband laying there on a hospital gurney, arms and legs moving involuntarily, I could hear myself tell him that it would be okay even though I didn't feel that way at all. I told him that I loved him; I told him to hang on. There was a nurse I recognized from the hospital where he had had the transplant. She said how sorry she was, and I spoke the thing that wouldn't leave my head: "This wasn't supposed to happen."

I didn't know at this point whether Leigh would live or die. There was a private room just off the ICU waiting room where they let me be alone for a while, so I sat there with a box of one ply tissue and cold legs curled up under me on a hard hospital chair, trying to think. Our daughter was at home, two hours away from where she needed to be, which was with me. How would she get here and what was I going to say? How do you say that over the phone to a fifteen-year-old girl—that her father may die at any moment? There was no one I could call in my own family and no one in Leigh's family; they were all strangers to me. I tried to call Scott but couldn't reach him, so I left a message. Then I called a friend at my work who offered to pick up Brienne and bring her to me. In the meantime, Scott had heard my message and contacted Leigh's father and his sister. He offered them a ride to the big city and was shocked when they both turned him down.

Scott had known Leigh since they were kids, so, he knew his entire family. He had good memories of his time spent with them so he would likely have said they were close. He was also aware that there had been some problems between me and Leigh's family, but he didn't know the details or the extent of the damage. Leigh's mother had passed away a little over a year prior to this.

How does a family react to a tragedy like this after years of silent hostility towards the one who was left alone to hold up their brother and their son? I was in that ICU waiting room from the early morning hours and the only genuinely compassionate call that came from his family was from Leigh's oldest niece, Holly. Later, I received a call from Leigh's brother, but he made it clear that his concern was for Leigh alone, not for me. The final call came from Willie. On the surface, he sounded like he was devastated but, as always, my intuition told me it was insincere. The part of me that was desperate for some kind of normal was trying to take it as it was presented, so I was vulnerable and emotional in my conversation with him. By this time, my co-workers who had brought Brienne were sitting with us, sharing our grief and waiting for news. The neurologist finally came to tell us that they had stabilized Leigh but she said he wasn't out of the woods yet.

Any illusions I may have had that there must be some humanity in my father-in-law's heart were dismissed when my co-worker friend told me what was going on when she picked up Brienne. While his son was fighting for his life and I was going through hell, Willie had been on the phone with my daughter telling her that she was nothing like me. He pretended to care but, behind my back, he was filling my daughter's head with hateful garbage in an attempt to damage the bond between us.

I lost track of time at this point. Days and nights seemed to meld together during the countless hours spent in the ICU waiting room. The head surgeon who had overseen the transplant and who had reprimanded us when we left the hospital during the discharge debacle, came in his off hours to check on Leigh. What did I think about this man? Emotions were in a state of turbulence and it would have been easy to cast some blame. He was with us in the waiting room a couple of times and he admitted that he couldn't even look at our daughter. Seeing and hearing the guilt and distress on his face and in his voice, I told him not to blame himself. He wanted to have Leigh transferred back to his hospital so he could personally oversee his care, but this never happened. Instead, he continued to come and check on Leigh. I wanted to have him moved back home as soon as he was strong enough.

Leigh was still alive but he was a mess. He couldn't swallow, so he had a feeding tube down through his nose to his stomach. Instinctively, he kept pulling it out, so they had to strap his arms to the bed. There were times that his feet were bound as well. It was absolute torture to see him suffer this way, and the unanswered question that hung in the air was "Why?" Anna, the transplant coordinator, was choking back tears when she told me how sorry she was and how this had thrown everyone on the transplant team for a loop. They had never seen anything like it, and they had no clue why or even how it happened. They had used the clot busting drug when he had the embolism, but they couldn't give it to him again when he had the stroke because it would have killed him. The many tests they had done prior to the transplant gave no indication that this could happen, and there was no explanation for how the clot crossed over from the lungs to the arteries leading to the brain. He had an irregular heart rhythm, so one theory had been that perhaps he had a hole in his heart, but further testing showed that this wasn't the case. All in all, I thought to myself, it didn't really matter now.

In the turmoil that followed, Scott became a steady presence for Brienne and me as we tried to deal with everything. Even though I had known Scott through Leigh for many years, we didn't really know each other. He was Leigh's friend first and foremost. He had grown up with Leigh and his family, so that was his main perspective. He had been friends with Leigh's brother, Peter, and with his sister, Cate. Because he was observing everything up close, and he could see that I would have been dealing with this alone if he wasn't there, I wanted to tell him why. Nevertheless, I was nervous about confiding in him, believing that he had the wrong impression of who I was and wouldn't understand my perspective regarding the rift. I told Scott how bad things were, including how cold Peter had been when he spoke to me.

Scott could see how distraught I was, and soon afterwards he told me that he had spoken to Peter about his attitude. I was so grateful for Scott, immediately sensing that God had sent him into the circumstances to help me, to help us. To me, he was like archangel Michael—a protector and defender. He certainly had the stature, being almost seven feet tall. Almost immediately afterwards, there was a change in Peter's demeanour towards me. He reached out to me, offering the option for me to stay with his sister-in-law who lived in the big city. It was encouraging to be shown some kindness, but I had a hard time embracing it, knowing it was only because Scott had said something. If I could look at it from Peter's perspective, and leave my own hurt out of it, I could understand that the hostility towards me had taken hold a long time ago, and it was based on the influence of his father. Changing an attitude about someone, even when it's based on a lie, is like trying to change the course of the Titanic. As soon as Leigh was somewhat stable, I went home.

Having been on leave from my job for a little over a month, my employer's insurance company was pressuring me to return to work. To paraphrase the young lady from the insurance company, this was my husband's illness, not mine. Therefore, regardless of my doctor's assessment that I was suffering from Post-traumatic stress disorder, they were threatening to withdraw financial support. Furthermore, my position at work was unstable. I didn't have a permanent placement, and the assignment I had been on for the last few years was coming to an end.

Being at home with our daughter and prayer were the things that kept me going, but I was filled with anxiety. The thought of travelling on the high speed highway to see Leigh conjured up dread and the memory of my previous panic attack. Scott was still working full time himself, but he offered to take Brienne and me to the big city on Sundays. Another time, I went with my friend Joan, taking the train part of the way. The visits with Leigh were exhausting because they were so devastating. His condition was fragile and every time, before we entered his room, we had to put on smocks, masks and gloves.

We thought that music might lift his spirits so Brienne started to play a Guns N' Roses song on her i-Pad. The whistle and acoustic melody of "Patience" started to fill the room but instead of recognition or a smile, Leigh's eyes filled with tears. Rock music had been something he loved, but I could imagine maybe now it was like an arrow that pierced through the heart of a life that was gone. Leigh couldn't speak, couldn't swallow, couldn't move his body because he was paralyzed on one side, and his vision was impaired.

Amid all of it, I marvelled at our daughter's composure. It wasn't until we were coming home in the dark from one of our trips to see him, that I saw the pain break the surface.

I glance in the rear view to see the tears fall
As the radio plays
"Everybody Hurts"
And together we're a part
Of sorrowful synchronicity

It took two months for Leigh to be stable enough to be transferred back to the hospital at home. He was still barely functioning and I was at the hospital several hours every day to be his voice. Cate called me one night; it was the first time I had spoken to her in many years. It was a guarded conversation between the two of us, but she sounded kind and supportive, so I was grateful for that. On the other hand, the call Willie made was carefully crafted to appear sympathetic. He made the clichéd offering of "anything I can do" and I called his bluff by saying that I had a pile of hotel bills left to pay. You could have heard the crickets sing during the long silent pause. Then I just told him to forget it.

Willie would go to visit his son and upset Leigh by trying to force him to use a computer tablet. At times, Brienne and I would show up to hear Leigh yelling in distress because of Willie's persistent "help". Leigh had never in his life shown an interest or aptitude for computers, so it made no sense whatsoever that this would be of use now. I asked Cate to intervene with her father to get him to back off.

Leigh was on the stroke rehabilitation floor. He had some excellent and empathetic therapists, but his progress was very slow, and he was having physical difficulties that were preventing him from fully participating in therapy the way they expected or hoped. After Leigh had been there for about a month, the main neurologist made his assessment which was summed up in telling me to go on with my life. I was in shock that this doctor appeared to have written Leigh off already. After mulling over the attitude of the doctors for a while, I found myself more angry than defeated. All it did was make me more determined to fight.

One Friday afternoon, a nurse called to tell me that management had decided, against his doctor's wishes, to take Leigh off the stroke floor and move him to general medicine. They did it without consulting me and they made the move on a weekend so that I wouldn't be able to raise any objections with anyone during regular business hours. I insisted on speaking with someone to express my anger that they would deprive him of the specialized staff or equipment that he needed for stroke care.

It was even more frustrating because his therapists agreed with me that he had started making a bit of progress. A previous application to undergo specialized rehabilitation at a different local hospital had been rejected, but another one had been submitted by the therapists. Things were looking bleak, and I could tell that Leigh was giving up, so it was a well timed blessing to hear that he was finally accepted into the rehabilitation program.

However, this first piece of good news was countered by the misery and defeat I saw in the stone-like expression on Leigh's face.

Through tears I begged him, encouraged him and made him promise me to continue fighting.

Leigh was put into a large private room at the rehabilitation hospital, and, for the first time in a long time, I felt some hope. Compared to the acute care hospitals he had been in, the atmosphere was less frantic and more welcoming. Nevertheless, as time went on, I began to worry because Leigh wasn't progressing as well as expected. His inability to communicate was a huge issue and the medical professionals would look at me to interpret. Sometimes I could figure it out, but, I was often just as lost as they were. I was feeling a lot of pressure for Leigh to do well because the funding would only allow him to be in the stroke rehabilitation program for one month.

As the end of the month approached, a social worker came to tell us that Leigh needed to be put on a waiting list for a nursing home. Again, my mind was having trouble believing that this was real—that this is what it had all come to. I couldn't accept that Leigh would be completely dependent for the rest of his life. Desperate for Leigh to stay at the rehab hospital and have as much therapy as he could get, I was determined to make a case for Leigh with a new doctor who was assigned to him.

I was fighting for Leigh, but the strength didn't come from me; it was coming from a higher source. I was struggling with the weight I was carrying and the feeling that everything was out of control. At the same time, I was awakened to an appreciation for all the good things I had in my life—my daughter, my friends, a home and food on the table. My work situation was miserable and unstable, but something happened on that front that I knew was a provision from God. A position was offered to me at my workplace during a time when there were no permanent jobs to be had.

Shortly after Leigh's return, our daughter's sixteenth birthday and, after that, a milestone birthday for me as well. Harsh reality had crashed both parties, but our love for each other remained intact. Leigh tried to sing Happy Birthday with me to our daughter in a hospital hallway. And, for my birthday, Scott decorated Leigh's room with banners and balloons and gave me a card that Leigh had tried to sign.

Around the corner from that was Christmas, which, again, seemed to be a poorly timed celebration. Leigh was paralyzed on the right side of his body; he wasn't able to eat solid foods and he couldn't talk except for a few random words. Leigh's body had failed him, and the irony of ironies was that his pancreas was working—no more worry about his blood glucose levels. If I had a choice, I would have taken that worry back in a heartbeat.

There was a card that came from my cousin on my mother's side that read "Hope life is good for you guys…" I sent her a return card that said "In fact, things aren't so good, and my mother turned her back on me years ago…" I never heard back. When a Christmas card showed up in the mail from my mother, who I hadn't seen or spoken to in years, I was upset. She didn't know what had happened to us and I agonized over it in a conversation with my daughter. Brienne offered to call her grandmother and tell her. When my mother heard the news, her reaction was to ask how our dog was; she didn't ask anything about me or about Leigh. I collapsed on the sofa, shaking and crying as my daughter hugged me.

Chapter Three
Homeless

And you didn't understand
Why you couldn't leave
And it broke our hearts each time
Your daughter still in high school
Tells you about her essay
On homelessness;
And you nod your head to say
That is what you are.

A heavy darkness settled in and around us and the world was permanently changed, although I hadn't yet given up on the idea that it could go back to the way it had been. Life was now divided in two: before Leigh's stroke and after Leigh's stroke. Only two months earlier, Leigh had been working full time. He was a guy who loved power tools, pick up trucks and walking our dog, Ruby. Now, he required a feeding tube and he'd been in four hospitals since the transplant that was supposed to make his life better.

In my bones I had aged a couple of decades in the two months since his stroke. My daughter gave me a journal to write in, and, even though I had never been one to keep a diary, I thought it might help me unravel the tangled mess of thoughts and emotions. The hours, days, months that I spent in hospitals and the fast approaching date of my return to full-time work were taking their toll. When a day came that I didn't visit, I would feel weighed down with guilt. At the end of November 2013, I wrote *going out lately, amongst the crowds of Christmas shoppers, I feel even more apart and alien than usual. It all feels so superficial and frivolous. The only thing that seems real to me is the sadness, with brief glimpses of joy here and there in nature, my daughter and our dog.*

I was looking for God everywhere, in any good thing that came our way, and His provision would show up at the lowest points. Leigh's co-workers raised money for us through a raffle and said prayers for him. Our neighbour, Mike, was coming to read to Leigh and another neighbour was clearing snow out of my driveway. Scott was visiting regularly, which relieved me of the pressure to be there all the time. Even Leigh's sister and father were visiting from time to time, and, despite my uneasiness about them, I was grateful.

Scott's sense of humour, easy going demeanour and generous spirit were like medicine for anyone around him and this was especially true for Leigh. Scott's entries in the visitor log often made me smile when I imagined Leigh in a good moment:

October 23, 2013. *The guy was in great freakin' spirits tonight…we bantered back and forth, laughing so hard the nurse came in to see what the problem was. We had Malcolm (the patient in the next bed) laughin' his ass off. Good visit.*

November 1, 2013. *As you can see, Leigh and I had a fun night! He took one look at my face and I told him it was Movember [a month when men shave their mustaches to raise awareness for men's health issues], and he wanted in on it. I asked several times, and he was quite adamant that he wanted his stash off, so PRESTO!!! I look forward to bringing Ruby up tomorrow!!! Happy thoughts, good times.*

The following day, Scott, Brienne and I brought Ruby into the hospital to see Leigh for the first time in months. Scott called our labradoodle the "happiest dog in the world." With her tail whip and butt wag, she had Leigh crying as he patted her with his one good hand.

To see Leigh without the mustache was strange because my daughter and I had never seen him without one. Leigh's short-term memory was gone and he didn't realize that he had asked to have the "stash" removed. He took one look in the mirror and made it clear he wanted it back.

Back when he was still in the big city, the evolution of "Leigh-speak" started with sounds or words that didn't make much sense. He would say "Or Nor" and then "Nord". Once, when Scott was visiting, he was showing Leigh as he played Yahtzee on a tablet. A full house came up, prompting the sound of a doorbell. Immediately, Leigh turned his head to the door and clearly said "Hello." Shocked and amazed, Scott asked him to say it again, but Leigh reverted back to his default, "Nord." The sound of the doorbell must have been the cue to tap into some deeply embedded language memory, but he was never able to duplicate it. Leigh's "Or Nor" and "Nord" phase didn't last after he left the big city. Back home, he eventually began saying some recognizable words like "yuck", "why", "one" and "sure". A phrase that he would say over and over again was "and so", which I'm sure made sense to him somewhere in that part of his brain that knew what he wanted to say but couldn't. One day he said "shit", and that word became a regular part of his lineup. You couldn't help but laugh every time he said it. The other side of this was the mounting frustration, for Leigh and for me, with his inability to understandably communicate something more complex. It meant asking endless questions, and I couldn't always depend on him to comprehend what I was saying; he could acknowledge yes and say no, but sometimes he would mix them up. I did my best to be patient but, at times, it overwhelmed me.

I wrote in my journal, December 2, 2013. *My visit with Leigh after work today wasn't the greatest. He was in a grumpy mood and agitated again because he expects me to understand what he is saying and no matter how many times I explain why I don't—that all he says are the same two words "AND SO"— he continues on and on and gets angry when you try to interrupt the endless "AND SOs" to ask a question so you have a hope of knowing what the hell he's saying!*

We were told that Leigh had apraxia and global aphasia which is the most severe form of the impairment. The damage to the left side of his brain had wiped out the language centre, affecting his ability to process information coming in and express things he wanted to get out. Initially, I was full of determination to see his speech restored. Even though he had speech therapy in hospital, I thought I could do more, and I used some of the money we were given to buy some language software. Even so, repeated sessions on the laptop with Leigh almost always ended in frustration.

On December 3, 2013, I wrote: *Just feel like crying today … took a break from visiting tonight but the hospital called to say that he fell trying to go to the bathroom. Apparently, he's OK. He'll never be able to come home unless a miracle happens…*

When I went to see Leigh the following day and tried to explain to him that he shouldn't be trying to go to the bathroom by himself, he became emotional and started crying. I was able to piece together that he was yelling because he needed to go to the bathroom and the nurse "shushed" him. He showed me where he had hurt his arm when he fell. It was shattering to see my husband, the man with the independent spirit, now so humiliated and helpless. Before Leigh's world blew up, I had been backing away. But now it was more evident than ever that I needed to be his voice, so I went to the administrator to complain about how he was treated.

The following day was better. When I arrived, a therapist was helping him play cards and he looked happier. Later, when I took him to the cafeteria, he was emotional, but this time it was because he was overwhelmed with the kindness of one of the nurses. The night staff had been spoken to after my complaint.

Leigh fell again leading up to Christmas, and this time they sent him to Emergency at the acute care hospital across the street. Again, the ambulance attendants, doctors, radiology technicians and all the various medical staff were looking to me as the interpreter and keeper of all Leigh's medical data. I did my best, but it was daunting, frustrating and exhausting. We spent nine hours at Emergency that time, and luckily there were no broken bones.

The days were like a roller coaster, a ride that had always made me feel sick even as a kid. On the one hand, Leigh was able to sit in a wheelchair and propel himself using his left leg and foot and he was finally able to eat and drink. But then Brienne and I were heartbroken when he started crying because he didn't understand why he couldn't come home with us.

Scott and Kristine were spending more time at the hospital because her mother had been admitted to palliative care there. They invited Leigh, Brienne and I to join their family for Christmas dinner in hospital. Leigh wore a Santa hat and drank a beer, and we all laughed and relaxed for the first time since the nightmare began; I ended up calling it the "best worst Christmas ever." It was the best because it was the first Christmas in many years where I was actually welcomed somewhere with my husband and daughter, and it was the worst for obvious reasons.

Since the stroke, I had had no choice but to interact with Leigh's family, and I was doing my best to put them all on a new page after what had happened, knowing that Leigh needed to see them. As expected, my father-in-law wasn't making it any easier with his oblivious behaviour. Managing to be in the same room with him for any length of time as we crossed paths was a testament to my willingness to try. I didn't like that Scott kept pushing me to keep Willie informed about any updates on Leigh's condition, as if I was the one wearing vindictiveness like a layer of skin. Understanding that he was trying to be neutral, I could appreciate that his perceptions of Leigh's family were inconsistent with mine, but I was hurt.

My life had been held hostage by the secrets and brokenness of other people, in my own family when I was a child and again through my marriage. And the one who should have stood for me, Leigh, had a blind heart and a hidden fear that prevented him from standing up for himself, let alone me. Who would believe that Leigh's father, with his charming facade, was the antithesis of what a father should be? Who would believe that he was the one who set the family example for hostility and indifference towards Leigh and me— invalidating and minimizing his son's health issues and my importance in his life.

Peter drove six hours to come see Leigh just after Christmas. When we crossed paths at the hospital, it was the first time in years that we had seen each other. I had spoken to Cate on the phone a few times, but we didn't get into the past. I knew she was aware of what her father was capable of, but I also believed that she was still well within the gravitational pull of Willie's orbit. Her assistance was needed, more than once, in managing her father. I was furious when a nurse told me that Willie had taken Leigh for a coffee before he was cleared for drinking liquids. My husband could have choked or aspirated. If I ever expressed anger about the incident around Leigh, he would get agitated and say "no, no, no." Most likely, Leigh indicated to Willie that he wanted to drink coffee. Nevertheless, the onus was on Willie to make sure it was safe to do so. So, there it was, my husband was still defending him even in his brain damaged state.

With Christmas barely over, I was sinking into hopelessness again. On December 28, I wrote *I feel like there is no end in sight— no return to "normal". I don't even know what the new normal will look like for us. We fade from the thoughts of most as they resume their lives…*

And on December 3: *I went late afternoon yesterday to visit Leigh. I was telling him how upset I was by the behaviour of another nurse on Saturday the 28th, and wondered whether I should complain about her. He was adamant "no" and when I tried to find out why, he would continue with his gestures and his "And Sos" with an angry tone and wouldn't let me ask questions to try and figure it out. I told him I didn't deserve his anger and I left. He was wheeling himself out the door of the room before I gathered up my things. I could see him wheel himself back to his room when I turned around to look through the double doors. I was so upset I went down to the main floor and sat in the lounge. I called Brienne. Then I called Scott and talked to him. He listened without judgement and I let out what I was feeling. He told me I was a great person—told me what I needed to hear—and it gave me strength to try again. I went back up and joined him in the dining area for his meal, and he was much calmer and he listened to me. I gathered that the nurses were spoken to because of my earlier complaint.* Later I was able to piece together that Leigh was afraid of backlash from the nurses if I complained.

The new year started off with some exciting and uplifting news. We met Leigh's new doctor and it was his opinion that Leigh could walk again—not well and not for any great distance—but the hope was there. It was exactly what I needed to hear after the government employee assigned to Leigh's case told me to get the application in for a long-term care facility. One afternoon, Scott called and told me that when he visited Leigh, he found him in the dark, just staring into space. Leigh was upset about the talk of putting him in a nursing home. Scott reassured him that I was doing everything I could to keep that from happening. Later that evening, when Brienne and I went to see Leigh, I pulled his wedding band out of my purse; I had been holding on to it since the transplant. I gave it to him and told him I would fight to keep him at the hospital as long as I could, to give him a chance to recover.

The first day in my new permanent administrative position was January 6, 2014: the stable job that God provided for me at precisely the right time. I had worked for twenty four years for a corporation in an administrative capacity, but the stability and certainty of that job had been diminishing rapidly. I was awe struck because the provision was so significant and, the improbabilities and intricacies involved in making it happen left no doubt in my mind that it was from God.

I was making prayer a part of my morning routine; it became fuel for the engine that faced a mountain every day. I was saying the serenity prayer, and I had created my own prayers: *God, give me the eyes to see, the ears to hear and the ability and the means to do thy will, help me always to see the truth in myself and others, protect me and the ones that I love from evil, ill will or intent.* Although, with that last part, perhaps I was looking for God to finally step in and say enough is enough. I asked Him to help me let go of the past and all the wrong done against me, to help me trust Him to take care of it and bring justice.

Leigh's first speech therapist, Becky, was our favourite. When I went in to see Leigh after work, she told me that he had been making efforts to make new people in the program feel welcome and was encouraging a woman who didn't want to eat. He was doing this with his trademark "And So" and gestures with his one good hand. This was one of the firsts in what would become a pattern. Despite his own severe deficits, Leigh was inspiring and helping others.

In mid-January we found out that Leigh would be allowed to stay at the rehabilitation hospital, but the bad news was that he could not stay in the stroke rehabilitation unit. He was going to be moved to another area called Complex Care, which would give him some therapy but not as much. Also, he would be going from a private room to a mixed-ward room, which was co-ed and could have up to four people. Another thing that hit me hard was the social worker saying that, even if Leigh did ever walk again, it wouldn't necessarily mean he would be able to come home.

As Brienne and I were getting ready to leave for the hospital, my cell phone rang. It was Leigh's voice on the other end and he said "Hey". I froze for a second. In that moment, it was like the last few months never happened and he was himself again. Oh, how my brain wanted to deny what was true but then reality was persistent. He continued "And So…And So…" I told him we were on our way to see him and he said "OK" and almost something close to "Bye" at the end. Brienne and I sat with him through his dinner with the intention of making it a short visit because I still had to go home and make dinner and go grocery shopping. Leigh was upset and angry that we wanted to leave, so we stayed longer. I knew that the hours in that place must have been torture. My heart was broken so badly for him, I swear I could feel it like shards of glass tearing me up inside. Yes, I believed that God was pouring into me the strength to do this, but I was physically and emotionally spent. And, at times I felt that it still wasn't enough.

January 21: *I took the day off work to spend time with Leigh and help him with the transition from Stroke Rehab to Complex Care. It was a very bad start. We were led into a room with a nearly naked old man right beside us—no curtain, no privacy. Across the room appeared to be two women, one looks almost dead. I put away his things. Leigh couldn't wait to leave the room and I couldn't blame him. I pray that he can hold on and not sink into depression. I think I would if I were him. Then, the new social worker we have to deal with seems like a phony baloney. He acts like he wants to help and then when you ask for it, he passes the buck. When he gave me the supposed reason for putting Leigh in that room, he said it was because Leigh has MRSA (a super bug) like the other three people in the room. I said that I didn't think that was correct, and I asked if they had tested him. He couldn't answer. In any case, he also said there were absolutely no private or semi-private rooms available.*

My gut told me that Leigh did not have MRSA. Therefore, they were exposing an immunosuppressed man to three people with a super bug! I questioned the social worker on protocol for testing, and he said that Leigh would have been tested once when he arrived at the rehab hospital (and he explained that is why Leigh had a private room in the stroke rehab unit) and once again when he came to Complex Care. Yet, he couldn't provide me the test results. I could feel the red hot flush of anger showing on my face, and I demanded that Leigh be tested.

On January 22 I wrote *Fret, fret, worry, worry all day long at work. I spoke to the doctor and head nurse, impressing on them my extreme concern about Leigh's current placement. They did the MRSA test today, but the results could take forty-eight hours. I hope he's negative. I went to see Leigh this evening and it certainly wasn't a boring visit. He claimed that he can suddenly see out of his right eye! Scott wanted to know if he was able to sleep after he got him some earplugs. Yes, I guess he could. I left for a few minutes to get laundry out of the car and when I came back, he was on the floor! He fell out of bed!*

And on January 24, *Triumph – Victory! Leigh's test came back negative, so he was moved into a private room! Suddenly the impossible became possible.*

Still and all, the room reeked and even though Leigh wasn't complaining, I brought in a diffuser to make our time there bearable. It was evident that being in a hospital setting was not going to be short-term, and nothing about the surroundings was a comfort. I wanted Leigh to feel us around him, so Brienne and I put together a collage of family photos and a large canvas with Ruby photos for his wall. I brought in Leigh's pillow and a blanket, and I also started the habit of bringing in a bunch of flowers every week.

While we are fortunate to be living in Canada because we didn't end up with massive hospital bills, the free care wasn't going to be free any longer. I filled out an application to be assessed based on my income and begged the girl in the finance department to keep the payments low. We had moved into a new home only four years prior and the mortgage was still large. Less money was coming in as Leigh's salary transitioned from short to long-term disability. I was worried but not panicked, telling myself that things could have been much worse, and in my gut I knew that God was in this with me.

Close to the beginning of February, I was sitting with Leigh in the cafeteria for a long while and I started talking about how the transplant was the catalyst that changed all of our lives. He didn't remember any of it—how he had wanted a new pancreas so desperately, how I was filled with fear leading up to all of it and the complications afterwards. Maybe his brain was still protecting him, but, hearing me tell the story brought him to tears. I was having a hard time myself, with the constant replay of events in my head, as if the answer to why this had to happen was in there somewhere.

God would not let it overtake me—the sorrow that felt like a bottomless pit. Instead, my thoughts turned to finding ways to lessen Leigh's suffering. If it meant trying something unconventional, I was willing to try it. This led me to Helen, a compassionate lady who practised biomagnetism—a type of energy healing that is done by placing pairs of magnets on the body. Because Leigh wasn't able to leave the hospital, and she wouldn't be allowed to come in for this kind of alternative holistic treatment, I drove the hour to her house to have the treatment done on myself with the intention of healing Leigh from a distance; I became, in effect, the antenna. It may sound far-fetched, but it has its basis in science using the principles of quantum physics.

The treatments were directed at both the physical and emotional states of her clients. Helen would scan the body for pH imbalances and place a magnet pair over the imbalanced area. The theory was that any area of the body that was either too alkaline or too acidic was left vulnerable to disease-causing pathogens. Neutralizing these levels would kill them off. Of course, I told Helen a lot about Leigh's condition, but I was amazed when she was able to detect specific problems he was having of which she would have no knowledge. The emotion part of the treatment was based on the Emotion Code developed by Dr. Bradley Nelson. The idea was that negative emotions become trapped in the body, causing imbalances that lead to disease. Helen found that Leigh had trapped emotions of frustration, anger, humiliation, pride and abandonment. When I heard her say abandonment, a surge of my own pain rushed through me.

February 10, 2014 read *Something remarkable—Leigh's occupational therapist, Sarah, called me today because somehow he managed to communicate to her that she should speak to me—instantly I knew it was because I had mentioned to him a few days prior that I wondered if she had started the process for him to get a wheelchair. I was awe struck that he remembered and communicated well enough to be understood.*

Compelled to do something to lift our spirits, I arranged to have a singing Valentine come to the hospital on February 14th. Becky had been practising with Leigh so that he could surprise me as well: he said my name! He had also learned to say "Thank you". My heart was full.

The following day, his occupational therapist told me that Leigh could feel the cold floor with his right foot! They were trying different wheelchairs with him to see which one would be best, and I smiled when they told me that Leigh wanted a red one. It was also around this time that Leigh started wearing a sling to keep his paralyzed right arm and hand from hanging like a half-broken branch.

Family Day was only a few days later, so Brienne and I spent a few hours with him; he was so happy to be with us that he was crying as we all got on the elevator together. Before his stroke, Leigh had never been one to show vulnerability; anger was the emotion I remembered seeing all too often. Brienne and I were both adjusting, with different perspectives, to this new and sensitive Leigh. My heart was softening towards my husband. My daughter, on the other hand, was having trouble knowing how to relate to him as her father because it was a role reversal: he was more like a child.

Later that evening his nurse called to tell me that Leigh had a seizure. Panic was rising up again. I didn't sleep well, and the feeling was all too reminiscent of those early days in the big city when life was hanging by a thread. When I went to see him he was in bed, in tears. The nurse said he had complained of feeling dizzy and she said he had tried to get up on his own and had fallen. I pleaded for him not to do that again, and I sat with him as he cried. After a while, he rallied enough to get out of bed, so I helped him into his wheelchair, and I took him to the top floor to sit in the chapel and look out the window.

How could this happen when he had been fighting so hard and had come so far? I had been used to the seizures before the transplant, but those were diabetes related and hadn't been a factor since the surgery. I read on the internet about late onset post-stroke seizures, and I prayed to God that this be an isolated incident, that he would be healed. He had lost far too much, and the working pancreas had been the cost. What happened to Leigh seemed like the ultimate lesson in being careful what you wish for. He had wanted the pancreas transplant, almost to the point of obsession. When you want something that much, it's time to pray for guidance and to be completely honest with yourself about motivations. But Leigh was blind. He didn't believe in God, so there was no thought of prayer.

Even when your desire appears to be reasonable, sometimes that thing that you want can take you down the deepest, darkest rabbit hole so far and so fast, there's no way out by the time you realize it was a mistake.

Chapter Four
Anguish and Absurdity

And so, yuck, shit.
Random words trickling down neural pathways
Fighting to come out;
We grasp at every sound
Never quite reaching the clog

I told Leigh that all he needed was the tiniest bit of faith—mustard seed sized—to see great things happen, and I was on a mission to give him that. I was making regular trips to see Helen, the biomagnetist, explaining it all to Leigh: what she said, what she found. He cried to hear me talk about it, and maybe it was just because of my focused determination to see him better. In any case, I believed the sessions with Helen were helping Leigh because his mind seemed clearer and more at peace. He was able to say a sentence (with some prompting): "Howw r you?" I was so excited I took him up to the fourth floor to see Becky where we shared some laughs and some tears. I kept saying how amazing the change was, that it was God's healing coming through Helen. Then, with perfect comedic timing, Leigh lifted his coffee cup as his way of saying that coffee was the answer to this miracle, and we laughed.

When Helen went through The Emotion Code treatment, it wasn't a surprise that anxiety and shock came up for Leigh, but the intention was to help release those emotions through me. She applied the same treatment to me and feelings of worthlessness and unreceived love came up. When I thought about it—my love being given but not received—it really seemed to sum up the theme of almost all of my most significant relationships, starting with my mother. Helen also knew that I felt taken for granted. I definitely had those feelings before Leigh's transplant, and from time to time since, but a lot of that had disappeared after Leigh's stroke. As I prayed for Leigh to be healed, my own heart was starting to mend; the anger I had toward him was disappearing and I knew this was where I was supposed to be.

On March 1, 2014, I wrote in my journal: *Brienne wants to get her nose pierced. She knows I don't like the idea, but I was willing to let her do it. She says it isn't because a lot of her friends are doing it; it's because she likes the look. Anyway, I know it's normal for her to want to express herself and I have to let her try things, but it scares me. It wasn't until we visited Leigh later that I realized exactly why. He pointed at his neck and I was reminded about the huge cyst that he had on his neck when he was younger. It was so bad, he had to have surgery to remove/drain it. It was GIGANTIC! He motioned with his good hand that the infection travelled from his pierced ear to his neck. When I asked if he had done everything correctly as far as disinfection/self care, he indicated that he did. Then I realized that I was afraid because I had "let" Leigh do something he really wanted to do one too many times, and now look at him…all he wants now is a body and a brain that work. I asked Brienne to think about it and if she really still wants to do it in the summer, then OK. She was very upset, and I know Leigh felt bad.*

Leigh was starting to make some noticeable progress. He called his sister for the first time and showed off for her by saying "Howw r you?" I was told by the therapist that he was making gains in physio; there was improvement with his transfer on and off the toilet and his sister witnessed him as he walked, with assistance, for sixteen feet. I was starting to think that maybe it was possible for him to return home some day. Despite these good things and the fact that I was grateful for them, there was no escaping the undercurrent of sadness. When I went to Helen again at the end of March, The Emotion Code showed "forlorn" as a trapped emotion for both Leigh and me. I couldn't save Leigh from this. We were suddenly apart and alone with no idea of where this was going. Then she came up with the word "forgiveness" as it pertained to me, and over the following days I started thinking about my mother.

I grew up the eldest of three children. My brother, Troy, was a year younger, and there was always an unspoken rivalry between us for an invisible top spot. My sister, Karen, was three years younger. When I was young, I remember there was fighting, both verbal and physical, between my parents. My sympathies were with my mother, and I was afraid of my father because I could remember an incident where he pushed her down the stairs.

We lived on a seventy-acre farm that had been in my father's family for at least a hundred years. It was surrounded by land that was cleared and settled by my ancestors. My dad worked the farm and my mother, who had been a teacher, stayed home after I was born. When I was little, living on the farm seemed like a paradise for me, my brother and my sister. We had wide open spaces to explore and play in—barns, fields, wood lots and even a river nearby. There were animals to name and farm equipment to ride, and we had each other to play with. But that carefree life didn't last.

One afternoon when we came home from school, my mother wasn't there. I was around ten or eleven when she was taken to a psychiatric hospital about an hour away. Nothing was explained to us about where she was or why; we just had to accept that she wasn't at home. There was an unspoken confusion and a tension in the air as the months went by, bringing us to winter. Our father hired a lady who came to the house to fix meals and clean every so often. And every couple of weeks, on a Sunday, we would make the trip to see my mother in that scary and enormous place.

I had never seen people like this, with glazed-over stares and incoherent rambling. The walk down the sterile corridors towards our mother's room seemed endless. We would sit there awkwardly and listen to her talk about ordinary things, like nothing was wrong. Sometimes she would show us a craft that she had made. Why was she here I thought? What was the point in her making a doily or a placemat? On one of the visits, we were brought into an office where my father had been talking to a young lady wearing a white coat. She closed the door and she asked us, one by one, with our dad sitting there, if we would rather live with our mother or our father. There was no explanation for why this was happening. I was sitting there paralyzed with fear, wondering what to say and thinking that I couldn't choose my mother with my Dad sitting beside us.

My mother had been gone for months and I remember the cold, sunny and snowy day we all made the trip to bring her home. The way I was feeling went beyond empathy; it was as if I could feel her pain myself, and all I wanted to do was make her feel better. We stopped at a diner for lunch on the way, and they had some giftware for sale. I saw this bobble head dog in a little basket, and I decided I just had to get that for her, so I begged my father to buy it because I had no money of my own. He wouldn't do it, but I couldn't let it go. The only thing of value that I had was a silver dollar that my grandmother had given me, so I offered to give it to my father in exchange for buying it. He didn't want to, but eventually he gave in. I was so excited just thinking of how it would make her feel, to see how much I cared. But, after giving it to her, all I saw was her blank expression. It meant nothing to her. If my child-self could have described how she felt at that moment, it would be like giving your heart and watching the person you gave it to look right through you like you're not even there.

> *A precious thing to give*
> *For the chance to make her smile;*
> *Bobble head dog in a basket*
> *Bouncy free and without care*
> *For the lofty hopes of a little girl*

The mother I had known before was different than the one who had come home. Eventually I came to understand that she had been subjected to shock treatments, which sounded to me like something out of a horror movie. I found it very difficult to comprehend how sending an electrical current through her brain, like some appliance you plug into an outlet, was anything other than cruel. Her personality seemed to be gone. There was no laughter and no intonation in her voice; it was like the world was one colour. The diagnosis was paranoid schizophrenia.

I believe that was the beginning of the division and disintegration of our family. From there, we just carried on with little to no communication about what had taken place. Eventually, Mom would stop taking her medication and Dad would arrange to have her taken, against her will, to the hospital.

My sympathies were with her for a long time, but a pattern emerged that gradually changed how I saw her. She was my mother, so she was the one I went to; she was my view of the world. From a young age she set me apart, building the foundation for a life alone. From not allowing me to attend birthday parties or forbidding me to make friends, to cautioning me against my own father, I learned to be afraid and I learned not to trust. The segregation didn't just apply to outsiders; she applied standards of perfection to me that were not expected of my brother and sister.

One time when I was with Troy and Karen, I made a careless and childish remark about our cousin, saying he was stupid. They went to my mother to tell her what I said. Instead of speaking to me about it and correcting me, she called our cousin's mother and told her what I said, in a private conversation, and apologized for how horrible I was. Over time, her treatment of me and the shame I felt settled deep into my psyche, wounding both soul and spirit. I turned inward, isolating myself in subconsciously believing I was worth less than others.

My brother was her favourite, just by virtue of being a boy; my sister became a tomboy because, on some level, she knew it would give her favour. Where was my father in all of this? Overall, he was a quiet man, but I saw bursts of anger that frightened me. I think he was in over his head and he was coping the only way he knew how. He was busy running the farm, which left the majority of the parenting up to her, despite her instability.

We were part of a small farming community, and we occasionally went to the small Presbyterian church down the road from the farm. I perceived people looking at us, whispering, judging, pitying, and it left me cold. Although I believed there must be something more, that God existed, He didn't seem to exist there. I had no interest in organized religion or the hypocrisy I sensed in all of it or the people around me.

Fast forward to the last time my mother and I had spoken, about four years ago, on the telephone shortly after Leigh's first transplant. Then, at least, she tried to sound concerned for our welfare. This time, she couldn't hide the indifference when my daughter gave her the news of our catastrophe. And, my brother and sister cared even less. Seven months after Leigh's stroke, I wrote a letter to my mother, but decided not to send it.

Mother: I know that none of you give me any thought (any good ones at least), but I need to say some things. Despite some despicable treatment, for most of my life I tried to overlook it and tried to have relationships with all of you. Unfortunately, or fortunately, depending on how I look at it, I've been forced to see the truth. The lies and manipulations from you, Troy and Karen, have made for a very confusing web to sort through. I'm sure I still don't know everything, but I know your intent, whether you were aware of it or not, was to punish me, harm me, crush me

I know that you suffered as a child (being molested by an uncle), and likely you were made to feel guilty. You probably never had anyone to talk to, to trust or to stand up for you. I believe that the molestation was followed by other horrible experiences, which ultimately caused your brokenness. Out of this brokenness came a degree of self-hatred that bred intent in your heart to inflict the same feelings of shame, guilt and isolation on someone—and that someone happened to be me. You probably weren't aware of what you were doing, but it doesn't make the betrayal any less. This is a primal betrayal—a parent betraying the one they're supposed to protect, their own child. The emotional abuse you subjected me to became the model of behaviour for my brother and sister. I'm sure you think it had nothing to do with you. You took every opportunity to shame me, to make me feel worthless. So, Karen and Troy learned from you how to deflect bad feelings of their own by lashing out at me. And when I was in a deep depression, you said to my face that I never should have been born....

You also told me that love doesn't exist, and you were right as far as you are concerned. Somewhere along the line, perhaps because of what you suffered as a child, you let the darkness take over the light that once was in your heart. Time and time again, I tried to show you love, but you threw it back at me like it didn't matter. I was never important enough. On the other hand, you treated Troy like some sort of perfect treasure—like he was far superior simply because he was born a boy. If you're honest with yourself, you'll see that your behaviour affirmed that if things had been the way you wanted, I wouldn't have existed, and Troy would have been your first born.

You've encouraged this idea or this concept that I received "more than my share." Yet, the same standards never seemed to apply to the rest of you. If there was understanding for hardship, it was for Troy or Karen or yourself—never me. The fact that I've had people to support—under incredibly difficult circumstances, to say the least—as well as myself, has been completely dismissed in your judgements. Neither you nor Troy has ever had to stand on your own, let alone support anyone else.

These were things that I wish I could have had the strength and the clarity to say long ago, when I was still trying to maintain relationships with my family, not fully realizing the damage I was doing to myself in the process. They were profoundly broken people who knew no better than to hurt me, but I was too confused and filled with shame to see it for what it was—abuse. It was the most insidious kind of abuse, whether you call it emotional or psychological; it's the kind not easily seen and certainly not well understood by those who have never experienced it themselves.

* * * * *

The rehabilitation hospital had been a blessing but there were things that came up that frustrated and angered me. I knew that one of the major contributing factors was likely hospital underfunding. But, at the same time, I believed some of it was just laziness and apathy. Almost every time I came in for a visit, my husband would be wearing dirty clothes. There was no excuse because I took laundry back and forth continuously, but I would notice he was wearing the same clothes for days in a row. I remember thinking to myself and saying to anyone who would listen, *"it takes the same effort to put on dirty clothes as it does to put on clean clothes."* Although Leigh didn't seem to care and it wasn't easy to change his clothes, I would do it anyway.

I complained about it more than once and it would improve for a short while, but then it would just go on as before. Leigh always seemed to have trouble sleeping, so I would keep asking that he be given some medication to help him sleep. It would be done on that day, but that note never made it on to his chart, so, there was no consistency. The lack of continuity and the ever-changing staff prevented the real caring that would have led to proper follow-through.

At times, I would have to hold my breath to wade through the awful smell of human waste on my way to Leigh's room. And, when I got to his room, there was usually a mess to clean up—from garbage and sticky spills leftover from meals to dirty toilet seats.

In the grand scheme of things, and in contrast to everything we had been through in the hospital system, these were nothing more than annoyances, and, I was worn down and tired of fighting all the time. Therefore, in the interest of maintaining my sanity and conserving energy, I gradually adopted a "pick your battles" attitude.

Despite its shortcomings, the rehabilitation hospital did have some wonderful features. One of its greatest assets was the large park-like setting behind it. It backed on to land with no buildings, just hills and forest, making it feel like you were in the country somewhere. Paved pathways weaved through gardens, leading to gazebos and benches. There were wooden picnic tables and big wooden chairs where you could sit, and the chipmunks would skitter through the gardens and sometimes even jump on to your lap. Anytime we were there in decent weather, we would take Leigh down to the cafeteria to get his usual "double, double" Tim's coffee and go outside. We would sit in the sun, thankful to be there together, silently replenished and embraced by the nature around us and the odd fellowship with the other people in their wheelchairs, alone or with their loved ones.

Before the transplant, Leigh was a man with a lot of simmering anger. When he did blow up, it was usually me in the line of fire. Now, in spite of everything that had happened, the anger seemed to be gone. He was the same in a lot of ways, with the sense of humour and the easygoing laugh, but now he had a child-like innocence about him. Leigh's right arm and hand were paralyzed, and the fingers would naturally curl in towards his palm. Our neighbour Mike, who I know God brought into our lives to help us, wrote this in the visitor's book: *Leigh made use of more new words than I've heard since first visiting with him…talked about his right hand and after several attempts to straighten his fingers on the arm rest of the wheelchair, he exclaimed "Stay!" This was followed by a chuckle (his sense of humour clearly well intact). When referring to his right leg, he used the word "Wow" a number of times, seemingly conveying some progress with the feeling/movement in his leg…and he even started counting mid-sentence, "One, Two" and always a few "Oh Shits" for good measure.*

In mid-April, the therapist called to tell me that Leigh walked forty-six feet with two people to assist. With the progress he was making, and the fact that Easter was coming up, we were planning to take Leigh out of hospital for the first time in about eight months! Scott came up with the idea of having Leigh come with us to their new house for a meal. So, I practised taking Leigh to the car and helping him transfer from the wheelchair into the passenger seat. And all was going well, until it wasn't.

Good Friday came, and in my journal, I wrote *this day was anything or everything but good.* It started out fine as Brienne and I came for a visit, took him down to the cafeteria for coffee and talked and walked around the mostly empty hallways of the hospital. Then I suggested a test run for taking Leigh in the car somewhere before the trip we planned to take on Easter Sunday. When we were about to transfer Leigh from the wheelchair into the car, Leigh's friends—

Scott, Erik and Andy—came by for a visit. Spirits were high in anticipation of Leigh's big day out. When they heard we were going to take Leigh out for a ride, they decided to meet us back at the hospital in an hour.

I drove us up the quiet side road that goes back behind the hospital, pulling off to the side. We just sat in the car with the doors open, taking in the sound of the birds and the wind moving the branches of the leaf barren trees. On impulse, I asked him if he wanted to go home for a minute to see Ruby and the house.

As we drove away from the hospital, Leigh was looking out the window in amazement. Even though he had grown up in this city and lived in it for decades, after eight months of solitary confinement, it must have seemed like another planet. As I continued to drive, he was becoming disoriented so he tried to cover his eyes by lowering his head. When we finally got to the house and I parked the car, Leigh appeared to feel better. We brought Ruby out to the car and he was so happy he cried.

Realizing that it was time to meet Leigh's friends at the hospital, I was driving back as quickly as possible. My anxiety was increasing as I began to realize that Leigh wasn't feeling well. Finally we reached the hospital, transferred Leigh into his wheelchair and rushed him into the building. With his one good arm, Leigh was grabbing at all the garbage pails in sight because he wanted to throw up. When we got back to his floor, he was given some nausea medication by injection and he was starting to feel better when his friends showed up again. As Brienne and I were about to leave, Leigh started to have a seizure. With my arms around him, trying to keep him from sliding out of his chair, I yelled for someone to get a nurse. There was a bit of chaos in the room; Scott said later that it reminded him of a scene from *Keystone Cops*. They called for an ambulance. Brienne was visibly upset, and Scott took her out to the hallway while the nurses administered some anti-seizure medication. Leigh was put into bed, with the seizure subsiding, but his leg was still trembling. He was taken to the acute care hospital across the street and while he was waiting on a stretcher in a hallway, he had another seizure. At least, it got the attention of the Emergency staff and they took him to a bed to be treated.

My daughter and I were shattered yet again. He had been doing so well, and now instead of Leigh's triumphant return to the world outside, it was a weekend spent in hospital with more uncertainty hanging over us. Leigh was sent back to the rehab hospital, and he was very tired when we saw him again. He seemed okay physically, but I could see that he was depressed. That night I wrote in my journal *I have to hold on to hope—what else is there other than a dark hole that's too hard to climb out of...*

I had been sent a letter from Leigh's employer that, in summary, said that they were letting him go by forcing a medical retirement. How was I supposed to think about the future when I was just trying to survive each day as it came? I knew he would never be able to work again but I didn't know what was going to happen next, and I was still trying to grasp how we were going to manage financially. My husband had not worked there for very long so I knew the amount of money for retirement would be small. I never intended to bring any of it up to Leigh, but on one of my visits an old co-worker of his showed up, and I told her about the letter. She was trying to help, but the discussion on the topic made Leigh cry. I believe that he understood enough of it to be upset about the impact on us. "Don't worry. We will be okay," I told him, even though I wasn't certain.

Leigh appeared to be giving up. The seizures had really knocked him down. I was doing my best to encourage him, giving him reasons to keep going. The biggest reason I could think of was the idea of coming home again. I hesitated, being afraid to promise more than I should. When I mentioned it to him, I told him that he would have to be more mobile and changes would have to be made to make the house accessible. Nonetheless, the seed was planted in his mind the minute I said that Brienne and I wanted him to be able to come home.

I confided in Leigh's therapists about my hope that he might become mobile enough for me to bring him home, and that seemed to push them that much harder to help him walk. I left work to come see for myself and it was nothing short of amazing. With a therapist on each side, and one following behind with the wheelchair, he got up and his left hand took hold of the quad cane. He was singing "And Soooo", staring down at his feet as I reminded him to look up.

Leigh's memory had been more impaired since the post-stroke seizures started, but one thing that he was not forgetting was the idea of going home. He was encouraged by all the buzz between the therapists and everyone else about his walking progress and he even indicated to Willie that he was being discharged. I wrote in my journal, *"I guess Leigh is certain that he's leaving the hospital and he's pretty excited over it. I know I've said things about wanting him to come home, that he needs to get a lot better, that I would need to be able to hire help and perhaps put in a stair lift. God, please help him to move forward—we can't take any more set backs."*

I started to reflect on our journey through the hospital system, and it had been like a teeter-totter between anguish and absurdity. If it wasn't one or the other, it was both. There were things that happened that left me wanting to laugh and cry at the same time. When Leigh was in the acute care hospital before he came to rehab, Scott recounted a period of time when Leigh would yell bloody murder whenever the nurses or therapists would pull him up and across to the edge of the bed. They just couldn't figure out why. Scott's intuition led him to ask Leigh if what they were doing was pinching his undercarriage, but the actual wording he used was less refined. Leigh pointed at Scott like he just won a prize and yelled, "Yeah!" It had never even entered their minds because the nurses and therapists were all women. Then there was the time where Leigh fell in a public men's washroom on the first level of the hospital and had no way to help himself. He was stuck there until he was found by the security guards. Another time, Leigh wheeled himself out front of the hospital, which sat on a hill, and decided to venture further away. Next thing you know, he's in an out of control wheelchair, flying down the hill. Someone must have found him and brought him back. Both Scott and I heard Leigh tell the story, but when I say "tell" it is not so straight-forward as you can imagine. We got the gist of what he was trying to say and, as always, we were both just shaking our heads in disbelief even though we knew it was a "Leigh thing" to do. Whenever my phone rang at home, especially late at night, I would get a sick feeling in my stomach and wince wondering what crisis was waiting on the other end.

There continued to be trips to the Emergency Department for falls. And I was frequently having to take time off from work to take Leigh to another hospital for follow-up appointments for his transplant, appointments with the neurologist because of his stroke, and routine appointments like the dentist. Then another complication developed with swelling in Leigh's right leg. It was swollen to the point where we could barely get a sock or shoe on and I was worried that he might have another blood clot. Thankfully he didn't have a clot, but he had something called post-thrombotic syndrome, which is impaired blood flow due to damaged veins and valves. So, taking him to a hematologist was added to my list.

There was a time when I would have thought to myself, with pride, that all I did for him was possible because I was strong. But now I knew how pointless it was to have derived my sense of worth from something that would have killed me had it not been for the grace of God. At that point, I was doing what I was supposed to do, and I was being given what I needed to do it. In the past I had relied on my own strength and independent spirit, pushing myself and martyring myself in my marriage when it wasn't giving me what I needed.

At the beginning of June, I was told that Leigh was being moved to another wing because he was doing better. I was nervous because he would not have a private room. It was semi-private, but at least it wasn't a room with three other people. We were relieved that Leigh's roommate seemed like a decent and kind man. His name was Don, and he only had a few months to live. He would help Leigh at mealtime by opening food containers or cutting food—things that Leigh couldn't do for himself with use of only one hand. He would look out for Leigh, like the time he called for help when Leigh was having a seizure in bed. When Don passed away, it was a reminder of how this place was like a fork in the road where you usually didn't get to choose the direction taken. One path was healing, restoration and release. The other was patching up, caring and preparing for the inevitable end of a life.

The idea of bringing Leigh home was looking more 'real' to me for a couple of reasons. Leigh was becoming increasingly unhappy. He pointed me in the direction of another patient who could voice what he was trying to tell me. This patient said that she had observed Leigh being treated with disrespect by some of the staff. Also, I found out that the cost of his care was going to more than double.

Even though I had this happy vision in my head of Leigh's homecoming, I was also worried. He was still having seizures, despite the fact that he was on medication for them. Troubled and not sleeping well, I was wondering if it would be too much for me.

For quite a while, I had been noticing that my husband didn't smell very nice, and he had this horrible crust throughout his hair and on his scalp. After asking one of the nurses how often he was bathed, I was told it was once a week on Sundays, which, to me, was bad enough. I decided to ask Don, and he said he didn't recall my husband ever being taken for a bath or shower! I was livid. That was the thing that clinched my decision to find a way to bring Leigh home: *I discovered that for the past eight months he has never been taken for a shower or bath and shampoo! It was the last straw for me. In an angry email, I blasted the social worker and the doctor. The social worker forwarded it to the Director, head nurse, etc., and the nurse coordinator told me it was a "miscommunication" and the entire tone was like they were sorry they got caught and were covering up. I accepted the apology, but I was still angry. I wrote to the health minister and the local member of parliament. The government won't give me enough money for care to bring him home to us, even though we want him here. There are waiting lists twenty years long for the two long-term care homes closest to us. The day programs are full. What am I supposed to do? Is the only option an old long-term care place you wouldn't put a dog in? I do not accept that.*

Chapter Five
All I Had

The "how" still wasn't figured out yet, but I was determined to bring Leigh home. There was a certainty in my heart that it was the right thing to do, but I was afraid. The team assigned to our case at the rehab hospital scheduled round table meetings for us to discuss the discharge plan because they weren't going to release him without one. Everyone who was involved with Leigh was there and that included Leigh himself. Even though he didn't understand everything being said, he knew it was about him and that it was about bringing him home. I worked full time and I was told that Leigh needed twenty-four hour care, but the government would only provide sixty hours per month of care. A representative for the government was also at these meetings and because I had not heard good things about the quality of the government-funded care, I was asking a lot of questions and looking for assurances on reliability.

They could see that I was troubled, and they repeatedly made the suggestion that I call on family and friends to help. Maybe that was a real option for other people, but for me it just wasn't realistic. When I pressed them on the issue of reliability, given that I had a full-time job, they hedged by saying that a support worker might call in sick or their car could break down, which meant I had to have my own back-up plan. Another concern for me was the character of the people they would be sending into my home, and I told them there needed to be consistency given that Leigh could not effectively communicate his needs to every new person that came.

I was trying to put together a plan and I made the assumption that I could at least schedule the hours they would give me however I wanted to. I discovered that I couldn't even count on that. Our situation wasn't typical, and we weren't the typical clients. The system was set up primarily for much older people in a different stage of life and also for those who didn't need twenty-four hour care. I needed to cover the time I was away at work. They told me that the care workers usually only came to a client's house in the morning for however long it took to get the client up and ready for the day and then again in the evening to get the client ready for bed. Also, I couldn't necessarily count on having the same people come every day.

My frustration was building because the meetings just seemed to produce more roadblocks. I was angered by the inflexibility of a system that is supposed to be about caring for people. In my mind, I wasn't sure what I was going to say at the next meeting but I had a spirit-driven determination to make it work. As a taxpayer, a portion of my taxes went to health care. I was being given an "allowance" of hours for care, but I wasn't being allowed any say in how I could use these hours or who would be coming into my home and caring for my husband.

The next meeting came and we went around the table with everyone giving their updates on Leigh. When it came time to discuss the discharge plan, I was hoping that the government-care representative would have reconsidered our specific situation and be willing to provide some better options. Still, I wasn't hearing anything different. When it came time for me to speak, I sat there in silence for a minute. Then, from a place within myself that I wasn't all that familiar with, I spoke with a calm boldness saying, "I am entitled to receive sixty hours of help per month. So why don't you just give me the money that represents and I will hire caregivers of my own choosing, people I can depend on to provide care at a time that suits our needs." Of course, they said it didn't work that way. Then I said, "Leigh and I have been through hell, and all I am trying to do is bring him home. How would you feel if this was you, if this was someone you loved?" My cheeks were flushed from the stress of the moment and there was silence. All eyes were upon me.

The meeting adjourned, but I was told shortly thereafter by the social worker that the government representative was willing to work with me to provide blocks of time according to what I needed, and they would endeavour to provide me as much consistency as possible with the workers they sent. Hallelujah, I was given a victory and, yes, I knew that God was in it.

I was taking steps of faith in preparing and planning, trying to think of everything. It was the end of the summer—almost a year since Leigh had had his stroke—and I had been shopping for good, used mobility equipment. Our house was not accessible, so the two therapists who had worked the most with Leigh came to assess the current layout and advise me on what was required.

Tapping into some retirement savings, my first major purchase was two stair lifts so Leigh could go upstairs to one of the bedrooms. At first, I thought he could share our king size bed again; I would just have to buy a side railing so he didn't fall out, and he could pull himself up with his one good arm. But I changed my mind. The idea of it just didn't feel right. Our entire world had changed, we had changed. And I had a feeling that the time alone in my bed at night could be my only respite. I bought a used hospital bed and set it up in the third bedroom I used as an office.

Our neighbour, Mike, came over to our house to install grab bars in the two bathrooms and a safety gate on the main floor. Scott came to install special hinges for the door to the main floor bathroom. These acts of kindness reminded me that God was still on our side when the heaviness seemed endless; it was these unexpected gifts that fed my faith and kept me from sinking.

It was good to have my brain focused on something positive, working out all the pieces of the puzzle to make Leigh's homecoming a reality. I was concerned about how I was going to pay for everything, so I pushed past my ambivalence about Leigh's family to ask his sister if she would watch him for a couple of hours on Monday afternoons. "It would amount to nothing more than a visit," I said. "I'll instruct the caregiver to take him to the bathroom before you come, so you don't need to worry about that." When Cate agreed, I was so surprised and grateful that I impulsively asked "Do you think Willie would do the same on Friday afternoons?" "Oh, I don't know about that," she said. "I'll ask and get back to you". To me, it sounded like it was possible but when she called back, she said "He said no, he might be going to Australia to see a friend." Leigh's father had always been one to put his needs and his schedule ahead of everyone else, so I wasn't really shocked, but I was disappointed. Conversely, for the outside world, he was skillful in his portrayal of the devoted father and family man.

After Leigh's stroke, when I tried to tell Scott about Willie and the rest of the bizarre family dynamic, it was a relief to unburden myself. As time went on and I started to trust Scott more as my friend and not just my husband's friend, it became more important to me that he fully understood. I sensed disbelief on his part regarding

Willie's true character. But I kept trying to talk about it because, inside, I was screaming for understanding, for vindication—trying to achieve it by my own effort. I wasn't far enough in my walk with God yet to completely let go and trust Him to deal with it. I knew that Scott had been shocked by Willie's refusal to accept a ride to the big city when his son was hovering between life and death. He was also thrown off by Willie blaming Scott and some other friends for "how Leigh turned out." Regardless, Scott still wanted to believe the best.

The government had contracts with some of the large companies that offered home care, and I was put off by my perception that these businesses were more about the money than about compassionate care. The money wasn't going to the workers who were actually caring for people because personal support workers are not paid all that well. As much as I wanted to minimize my costs, I knew I would have to pay for some private care. I decided to interview some smaller companies and I found a young lady named Brenda, who happened to live nearby. Almost immediately I knew I had found the right fit.

She was educated, compassionate and professional. Familiar with all the government bureaucracy concerning home care, she was willing to help find a solution within the budget I set. Her initiative in attending meetings with me at the hospital and speaking directly to the government representative to discuss options relieved a lot of the burden and stress.

Finally, all the details were worked out and the discharge meeting took place about a month before Christmas of 2014. I had taken a big step of faith and I believed that God had given me the determination and the way to bring Leigh home. A warmth came over me to think how he would feel, finally being in our home again after being away for more than a year.

It was pouring rain on a cold November day when I came to pick him up. I wheeled Leigh around to say his goodbyes, the last ones being to his physiotherapists. I pushed him to the car as quickly as I could, opened the passenger seat door, and started to try and help him transfer into the seat. In a rush and still uncertain of what I was doing, things got messed up. He ended up with his foot wedged and his body twisted like a pretzel, at which point he started yelling out in pain. I wasn't able to move him. He was yelling even louder, so I told him to stay put, as if he had a choice, and I ran back into the hospital for help. The physiotherapists came out, getting soaked themselves, and they managed to get him turned around and seated. I was relieved and past the point of caring that I was drenched. With Leigh safely in the front seat, I wheeled the chair to the back of the car to start the whole process of folding it up. Then it was the ole' heave-ho to lift and push it into the trunk. I ran to the driver's side, started the car and blasted the heat because we were both like a couple of drowned and shivering rats.

There were what seemed like a million things on the "everything to do with Leigh" list. I hadn't realized that the government would be sending everyone and his brother to my house—a nurse, a physiotherapist, a speech language pathologist and a government home care representative. I knew that the intention was to support and help, and I was doing my best to be patient and cooperative. Despite my effort, I ran out of patience after a late evening phone call from a nurse who said she would be coming to the house at 9 o'clock one morning and talking to Leigh about his medications. I explained that wouldn't be happening for a number of reasons: my husband wasn't able to discuss anything with her, I would be at work, he wouldn't even be awake at that hour and the caregiver wouldn't be able to help. Besides, I already had the prescriptions sorted out, so I didn't understand the need for the visit. She sounded like she was taken off guard and offended with my response but I was upset that she made all these presumptions and obviously knew nothing about us. Our home was constantly being invaded by strangers always asking the same questions, and I was seeing it as more of a hindrance than a help. After that call, I was so upset that I asked the home care nurse coordinator to stop the visits.

Leigh's blood needed to be monitored on a regular basis, so I arranged for a lab technician to come to the house every couple of weeks. In survival mode, I had to be on the ball with all the details which meant there was no time to dwell on thoughts about how tired I was. Regardless, I realized that God was making a way for me to handle these things. He had provided me a job that included a manager who was sympathetic and allowed me flexibility in my schedule.

No matter the outer turmoil, and no matter how things had changed, being together again as a family was like peace in the middle of a storm. We were adjusting to a new routine; even our dog, Ruby, found her happy place with her head draped over Leigh's paralyzed leg on the ottoman. With Leigh being in another bedroom, I found myself listening and sleeping lighter like in the days when I had a baby in the house. He couldn't take himself to the bathroom, so he used a urinal at the bedside. Many nights he would yell out "And So", and I would get up to empty it.

The speech therapist that came to the house didn't pull any punches when she said that Leigh's impairment was so severe that there wasn't much that could be done to assist him in recovering more speech. I wasn't surprised by it because he had reached a plateau in his progress at the rehab hospital. Brienne and I had tried with him as well. First it was the speech software I bought, which didn't really work out. Next were the flash cards with simple words and pictures from an educational store for kids. We would repeat the same words over and over, showing him the card but the most that came from the effort were a lot of laughs. I showed him a picture of a bear and he said the word "bark". Also, without the regular physiotherapy he had been getting at the hospital, I was resigned to the fact that most of Leigh's time would be in a wheelchair. The only time he would use his legs would be to stand and pivot onto a seat.

I had taken a few days off work to get a routine established with Leigh and to deal with all the home visits. One of the visits was with the personal support worker who was being sent in by the government. Her name was Peggy, and my impression was that she was a little rough around the edges, but she appeared to be kind hearted. My concern was about consistency and she told me that she would be the one coming, at least for the month of December. Anyway, right off the bat, there were problems. One day I came home at lunch and there was a man there I had never met. His name was Robert, and as I spoke to him, I began to feel more at ease because I sensed he was caring and professional. In speaking to both Peggy and Robert, I found it curious that they worked for a different company than the one which held the government contract. That's how I discovered that the caregivers were sent by a sub-contractor. No wonder the system came across as any other business concerned with money rather than people.

The following week, the phone rang at six thirty in the morning as I was getting ready for work. The company that held the government contract said that they couldn't send anyone to care for Leigh that day. I just couldn't fathom how a large company like that, which sub-contracted work out to another large company, couldn't find one person to cover a period of time that I had been promised. I started documenting these things and sending them to the management contact for the government care. At least she was sympathetic and concerned with doing her best to work with the agency to prevent this kind of mishap. Intuition told me that this wasn't the end of our problems. My morning prayers and daily talks with God were sustaining me, but I was still holding on to a lot of stress.

Scheduling some time off around Christmas, it was a relief to finally catch my breath and enjoy just being home. Scott came to the house with a cookie recipe that he made every year. This almost seven foot tall gentle giant was baking cookies, singing, joking and involving Leigh in the whole process. Scott could make Leigh laugh like no one else could. And from the moment he stepped into our lives to help, because there was no one else who was willing or able, I knew that God was using him, and it didn't matter that he wasn't a believer.

It was a day or two before Christmas, and I was taking Leigh to an appointment at the hospital to have some growths removed from his forehead. Transplant recipients are more prone to cancer and this was a form of skin cancer. The surgeon administered a local anaesthetic and started cutting away. As this continued, I started to notice that Leigh's body was quivering and I became concerned. I was reassuring Leigh, resting my hand on his leg as I mentioned it to the doctor who found it strange as well. Relieved when the surgery was over, I quickly took Leigh home and upstairs to sleep.

We spent a quiet Christmas Eve together watching *It's a Wonderful Life* before I started sending Leigh up the stair lift to go to bed. There were two lifts because the staircase took a turn near the top with a small landing for the transition. Leigh had reached the landing and I was close behind when he started to have a seizure. I ran up to keep him from slipping out of the chair, yelling at Brienne to call our neighbour Mike for help.

Mike had been asleep but he didn't hesitate to rush over. By the time he arrived, the worst of the seizure was over. Nonetheless, Leigh was disoriented and he was too much dead weight for me to lift. Mike and I managed to get him the rest of the way upstairs and into bed. Neither of us was absolutely certain if we should be seeking medical attention, knowing that any visit to the Emergency Department would mean many, many hours of waiting. It wasn't even just the waiting that was a consideration for me, it was the fact that Leigh was immunosuppressed and taking him to the Emergency Department was like taking him to a germ factory. Oftentimes with Leigh, I was making judgement calls based on a combination of intuition and common sense. I believed the seizure had been less than five minutes long, so I decided it was best for him to just sleep.

The experience shook me up. The following day and for the rest of that week, I noticed that Leigh was significantly weaker. It was difficult to get him out of bed and ready in the morning; taking him to the shower and getting him in and out was physically demanding. I didn't think I would be re-considering my decision so soon, especially after fighting so hard to bring him home.

I talked to the government-care representative who also dealt with placements in long-term care facilities. Of course, the decision was mine, but she encouraged me to consider taking a placement in an older home, perhaps even outside the city, to lessen the wait time. Waiting lists were years long for the newer facilities, but I wasn't willing to put Leigh just anywhere. I wouldn't be able to afford any private rooms, and the standard rooms in the older homes put four people together into a single room. In the newer homes, only two people shared a single room, so I decided that would be the only tolerable scenario. I wanted something close to our house as well. Years prior, we had watched a building going up in our neighbourhood, wondering what it was. When we realized that it was a nursing home, we never could have imagined that this building would be part of our near future. He had already been on the waiting list for a year with no estimate on when a spot would be open. Even so, after a lot of thought, I decided that this home was going to be the only acceptable option for us.

The logistics of how to let caregivers into the house had been a real puzzle for me. I would be gone to work already, Brienne would be already on the bus to school and Leigh would be upstairs asleep and couldn't get to the door anyway. It made no sense to provide a key when there were many different caregivers so I installed an electronic keypad just outside the garage. Caregivers could access the house through the garage. The arrangement was working until, one morning, my intuition lead me to check my email while at work. It was from the sub-contracted company that Peggy worked for and they said she couldn't access the house because the keypad wasn't working. Rushing home, I was grateful to find that Leigh was still asleep. After testing the keypad myself, it worked, so I was skeptical. Earlier in the week Leigh's right toe had been cut pretty badly while Peggy was lifting his leg to get him in and out of the shower. I knew how difficult it was, but I wondered if this was Peggy's way of opting out of looking after Leigh. What I was really upset about was the fact that he had been left alone for so long and no one called me. If I hadn't checked my email, he would have been left alone all day, trapped in bed.

Looking for ways to manage my stress, I arranged to take every other Friday off work, unpaid. I was still paying for private care in the afternoons, using that time to run errands or give myself a break. However, sometimes I would come home on a Friday and Leigh's father, Willie, would be there. He had the nerve to dismiss the private caregiver that I had paid to be there—this after he had refused to help on Fridays.

As I was almost ready to leave work one afternoon, a call came from the medical monitoring company saying that Leigh's necklace had triggered an alert. That was always my biggest worry—that gap of roughly half an hour, on some weekdays, between when the caregiver left and either myself or Brienne came home. With a vague mental image of the catastrophe awaiting me, I rushed in the door and up the stairs. I didn't know that Brienne had already arrived home from school and as she approached the house, she could hear her father inside yelling bloody murder. In an attempt to get to the bathroom by himself, he ended up on his back on the floor of the master bedroom. Again, Brienne called neighbour Mike for help and the two of them managed to get him across the floor and seated on the toilet.

Our daughter was only seventeen and she was trying to get through her final year of high school, so I was doing everything possible to avoid putting her in the position of being responsible for looking after her father on her own. On weekend mornings, there were times when Leigh would call out when I was in the shower or outside walking the dog. Brienne would wake up and just hope she could manage the problem or that I would be back soon. I couldn't leave the house until I got him up and out of bed, toileted, showered, dressed and taken downstairs for breakfast. It was a routine that usually took about an hour and a half to two hours. It took even longer when he didn't want to get up. Then, I would plan what meals to make, leaving Leigh with Brienne while I shopped for groceries. He would watch television, she would be busy with homework and I would leave feeling pressured to rush and get back home. The government-care representative approved a few more hours, so I asked for some help getting Leigh out of bed, showered and brought downstairs on Saturday and Sunday mornings. I wanted someone that could take care of these things while I quickly went out to grab groceries and a coffee.

After a couple of months, I was pushed to the breaking point again. I did whatever I could to avoid complaining because contemplating the conflict felt like it could be that "one more thing" that might just tip my little life raft over. I imagined that this was exactly the way many caregivers feel. I understood how people can find themselves at the mercy of a health care system just trying to deal with whatever crisis is in front of them, not having the energy to correct all the wrong things in their way. More than once I would be waiting for a caregiver to show up on a Saturday and no one would come. Or, they would send a complete stranger and I would have to explain and demonstrate everything for them, leaving me to wonder what good it was doing. I wasn't allowed to communicate directly with the sub-contracted company that was sending the caregivers to my house. One time when I did look up the number to call them to discuss scheduling, I was reprimanded by the administrator of the company that held the contract. I had followed their protocol, being as understanding and patient as anyone could be under the circumstances but when I started to experience increasing rudeness and condescension, I reached my limit. I felt compelled to share my experience and make a formal complaint to a government manager in charge of the contract. The only way to change things that are wrong is to be a voice, even if you're the only one. You've done your part and you pray for God to do the rest.

After all that, I decided the money wasn't as important as my peace of mind. It would be well worth the extra money to pay my private caregiver to come for that short period of time on the weekends. At least then I could count on someone showing up and that the person would be familiar with Leigh.

Finally, things were more stable with regards to care. I was satisfied with the caregivers who were coming, and they all genuinely cared about Leigh. He was forever saying "Thank you", just so gracious with everyone who came to look after him. I was feeling guilty about the thoughts I was having—how I was feeling worn down and discontent within myself because I wasn't seeing any end in sight. Resentment was creeping in. My life had become this tiny little box, and, if I was honest with myself, it had been this way for a long time. It's just that the box had become even smaller over time. I knew that this trapped feeling extended to our daughter as well. But Leigh was in the most confining place of all, and that was the heartbreak for all of us, especially him. I knew that he loved us, but he wasn't happy. I noticed it most on the mornings when he didn't want to get up, when he was being difficult. I didn't want to imagine the torture it must be to have such an independent spirit and not be able to do anything.

One Sunday morning when I trying to move Leigh from the toilet over to the shower, his leg gave out and I didn't have to strength to hold him up. It was all I could do to shift his weight to the wall and help him slide as gently as possible to the floor. However, as hard as both Leigh and I tried, we couldn't get him up off the floor. Leigh was naked and I threw a towel over him, having no choice but to call our daughter out of bed to help us. I think that was the moment I knew I had to seriously start praying for a place to open at the nursing home. I had spoken to Leigh about it more than once, both of us in tears. Even though it was obvious his brain was damaged, and he didn't understand all things, it never ceased to amaze me how much he did understand.

Not long after that came the call that there was a bed available at the home in our neighbourhood. Even though I knew this was what we had to do, guilt and fear were making me unsure. Not ready to to give an answer right away, I took the twenty-four hours that they give you to think about it before they move to the next person on the list. I called Leigh's sister to tell her what was happening and I was relieved when she understood the reasoning behind my decision to let him go. I called just within the deadline to accept the offer. However, his placement would be delayed because of a flu outbreak at the home. I was relieved that we had more time to adjust to the idea. Leigh had been at home with us for six months and although this wasn't what I had hoped for, I now saw that it was like a necessary piece in a puzzle that you're taking apart rather than putting together. What was left was the gratefulness I had for that time. Another phase of this journey was about to start, another step of faith into the unknown and another step away from what was.

Chapter Six
The Hen House

For losses have not corrupted
The best part of your heart;
No need for you to prove yourself
No room for pretence in this place
Where time means as much
As the clock on the wall that stopped long ago

I brought Leigh to Henway Home on a Monday at the end of April 2015, but I soon came up with my own name for it: the Hen House. My husband wasn't fighting it, but there was a bewildered kind of deer-in-the-headlights look about him as we were shown to the tiny room he would share with a stranger. As for me, I was carrying a mixed bag of emotions—sadness, anxiety, guilt and relief. One of Leigh's private caregivers came with me to help with all his clothes and personal items. I knew that she was very fond of Leigh, and when it was time for her to leave, I thought I saw a flicker of disapproval in her eyes. Perhaps I was just seeing the reflection of my own guilt. I was searching my mind for the positives to subdue the bad feelings. First impressions were good; the home was newly built, so it appeared to be clean and modern. The staff appeared to be friendly, and they offered to give him a bath in the whirlpool bathtub as I was getting ready to leave. I made sure to tell him I had noticed that they had something on the menu for dinner that he liked: lamb chops.

I left the home telling myself that it went better than expected, that everything was starting off on the right foot. Even so, all of that was out the window when the phone rang at midnight. The staff at the front desk dialled my number and put Leigh on the phone. I could tell that he was upset, but of course, there was no way to know why except to ask a million questions and hope I was on the right track. It had something to do with his roommate's snoring and not being able to sleep. The social worker left me a voicemail the next day and she said there had been a bit of a rumble between Leigh and his roommate, Charlie. Leigh had turned on his television to try and mask Charlie's snoring but this woke Charlie up, at which point he started shaking his fist in anger.

After work, I came in with some earplugs and then I brought Leigh home for dinner. One of the big challenges was Leigh being understood, especially in light of the conflict. The social worker was asking me if he was going to be getting more speech therapy but I told her we had already exhausted that avenue. She talked about making up a communication board using symbols that he could point at. Intuition and experience told me that it wouldn't help. They had already tried that sort of thing at the rehab hospital, without a lot of success. There was no possible way to come up with enough symbols to cover every possible scenario. And, often, Leigh would confuse his yes or no answers.

Cate visited Leigh on his second evening at Henway Home, and he was upset because Charlie was deliberately changing channels on his television while he was watching it. When the ladies on duty were not able to understand him, Leigh was pretty angry. Cate explained things to the staff and managed to calm him down. Soon after, I bought some headphones for Leigh so he could listen to his television without disturbing anyone.

Brienne and I both had a bad feeling about Charlie before Leigh's trouble with him started. He never acknowledged us other than to glare. It was difficult enough making this transition, and I was becoming worried because Leigh was pretty helpless in his wheelchair with only one good arm and hand. Charlie, on the other hand, was a big man with no mobility problems. I asked that Leigh or the roommate be moved, but I was told that the wait for another bed could be a while. In the meantime, the social worker assured me that their behaviour support team would work with Leigh and Charlie. I really liked the social worker; she was a very kind person, but I could tell that she was following an internal set of rules that were skewed in favour of the home's financial priorities. Still and all, common sense would have been to separate my husband from Charlie as soon as possible.

The situation with Charlie was escalating quickly, and it was frustrating trying to determine what Leigh wanted to say. I questioned him on a weekend that he was home, and tears welled up his eyes when I re-stated what I thought he was trying to tell me. Charlie was mimicking Leigh, using some of the phrasing and words that Leigh used.

Sending Leigh to the nursing home was supposed to alleviate stress and burden, but this ongoing conflict was a ticking time bomb, and the fact that the home was reluctant to do anything about it, was making me question my decision to put him there. I often went to Henway after work to bring Leigh home for a few hours, as well as bringing him home on weekends. I was no further ahead, as far as having a break for myself, than I was when he lived with us. To top things off, I was paying the full rate for a basic room which was almost double what I had paid at the rehab hospital—far more than what I had anticipated.

Charlie would laugh at Leigh and make fun of his speech impairment. He would also change channels on the television in the central lounge, even when several residents were actively watching something. Leigh pointed it out and Charlie retaliated by kicking him. The staff had alerted me to that incident because Leigh had tried to communicate it to them but none of them had seen it happen. They said that it didn't appear to have been a serious kick, that they couldn't see anything on Leigh's leg. Nevertheless, when I brought him home a few days later, I noticed a bloody scab on his leg.

Back at the house one afternoon while Brienne and I were just about to have dinner, we heard something outside the house that sounded like banging. Brienne looked through the frosted glass at the front door.

"It's Dad!" she exclaimed.

"What the ___!" I yelled and ran out the front door. Leigh was in his wheelchair in the driveway. Soon after, a car pulled up and a lady in uniform came running out. She was from Henway Home. I explained to her that I was his wife, but I wondered how Leigh had managed to escape the nursing home with no one noticing, making it with one good leg to propel himself in the wheelchair all the way to our house. She said that someone in one of the town houses across the street had seen him and alerted them. I was still trying to process the whole thing as I told her it was okay for her to leave and that I would bring him back.

There was no mistake that Leigh's great escape was a result of the abuse at Henway, and I wasn't sure what to do. To bring him back home would mean setting everything up with the government care again, and re-living the agony that led us to the decision to let him go in the first place. Also, it would mean starting the clock again on waiting for a placement somewhere else, and I didn't have a clue where to send him that would be any better.

Not even a week later, Leigh escaped again, ending up in our driveway. Henway was located in our subdivision, about a fifteen minute walk for someone who had no impediments, but I could only imagine what it would be like with one good leg and a wheelchair. When I questioned him about it, especially how he could possibly navigate the curbs where the sidewalk ended, he indicated that he was propelling himself on the road because he didn't like the bumps and cracks in the sidewalk! I was alarmed just visualizing how dangerous it was but, then again, it was a typical "Leigh thing" to do.

I understood why Leigh was doing this, but I was worried that he would get hurt, so I firmly told him he had to stop doing it. Other residents who were mobile were free to leave and come back into the nursing home, but they had to know the code for the keypad to get in and out. Leigh would just follow other people in or out and that is how he managed to escape. I didn't want Leigh to be on lock down where he couldn't get outside at all, so I just hoped that I had gotten through to him. At my wit's end, I found myself writing a long email to the home administrator one Sunday around midnight. At the end of it I wrote, *There is no way I would be able to articulate in a way that anyone could come close to feeling what we have felt. Mere words would never scratch the surface. In order for my husband, my teenage daughter and me to have some peace at last, would you please separate these two before something awful happens. Please find him a room mate who has a kind and gentle demeanour like he does.*

A few days later, they finally moved Leigh out of the room and into another one a few doors down the hallway. I was relieved, but still concerned because they would continue to share the same common areas. Leigh indicated that on the morning he was being moved, Charlie tried to punch him but missed. Right away, I sent an email to the administrator saying that I thought this should be reported to the government and that the home should be separating and segregating violent residents. The next day I met with him in person to discuss everything. Even though the administrator was tight-lipped, citing privacy concerns, I had heard enough from others, unofficially, to know that Charlie had caused some trouble before with other residents.

I took the administrator at his word that they were prepared to take appropriate action internally to deal with my concerns, so I dropped the idea of reporting the incident to the government. I just wanted peace and I was hoping that the move to the new room would be the answer. Horror stories had been in the news, from time to time, for years about cases of abuse in nursing homes. I just never imagined that I would be in the middle of one myself. Surely after this incident, the administrator must be taking me seriously; he must have known I wasn't someone unaware or unconcerned with what was going on. I wanted to give them another opportunity to handle things because it would be the quickest resolution, knowing that any government complaint would be a time-consuming process.

When Leigh's friend Erik came for one of his regular visits about a week later, he walked in on the next disaster. I only found out later when the social worker called me at work to tell me that Charlie had punched Leigh, but this time he didn't miss, and he broke Leigh's nose. Fortunately, Erik went with Leigh to the hospital, so I didn't have to leave work, but I was a nervous wreck the entire day. When Erik called me from the hospital, I was just sitting down in the dentist chair for a dental appointment. He assured me that Leigh was all right, but they had to re-set his nose. It wasn't until I hung up that I realized that I forgot to ask if they were giving Leigh any freezing or anaesthetic. I had discovered, after Leigh's seizures at Christmas, that the adrenalin component in the anaesthetic can affect some people. So, there was that worry as well—that Leigh might have seizures after all this. In the meantime, Charlie was sent away to a psychiatric facility. The social worker assured me that he would not be allowed back at the home and they had filed a report with the police.

I hated that this happened, but at least we didn't have to worry about Charlie anymore. Erik was keeping Scott apprised of everything that was going on during that incident. I knew that Scott was very upset. He called me at home on the day it happened, telling me that I had to take action. We ended up arguing because he wanted me to call the police myself, and he said that I shouldn't be accepting what the home said about filing a report. Normally, Scott was supportive and encouraging, but his emotion and concern regarding Leigh was coming through as anger directed at me. Even though I knew that the home had not handled things well, I was sure they wouldn't blatantly lie about filing a report; they would be breaking the law if they hadn't filed one. It hit a nerve with me because I was still trying to cope with guilt, and he left me with the feeling that I wasn't doing enough. Even though I had work early the next morning, I needed to prove him wrong, so I stayed up until two in the morning waiting for the police to show up to my house. The officer confirmed that the Hen House had filed a report and I was relieved, not just because I would be able to tell Scott, but because it put to rest any of my own doubts.

With that ordeal behind us, I was finally starting to feel more at ease. Leigh's new roommate, Joe, seemed to be okay—at least he didn't give the impression of being violent. He had a bible on his nightstand and family pictures all over the wall, so I took that as a good sign. After what had happened with Charlie, I asked the social worker if there was anything I needed to be worried about with Joe. She said he had dementia, but apparently he wasn't violent, so I accepted what she said. Then, only a few weeks later, as we were taking Leigh around the building to sit outside one summer evening, he tried to tell us something. I wanted to misunderstand what I thought he was trying to say. Joe yelled at Leigh and shook his fist; it had something to do with the bathroom. I was having a bad feeling already, but I suggested to Leigh that maybe Joe was just having a bad moment or a bad day.

Now that things were more stable, it was time to deal with the problem of how much we were paying for Leigh to be at the Hen House. I was sure that it was just a matter of sitting down with the home's finance person and providing proof of income, just as I had done when he was at the hospital. Before I made the final decision to put Leigh into care at the home, I had expressed my concerns about affordability to any of the government representatives I spoke with. They all led me to believe that I would receive a rate reduction, the same as at the rehab hospital, based on income and the fact that Leigh had a wife and a dependent daughter. But, two months later, after having taken my complaint to a regional manager for the government department in charge of long-term care, I found out that I would have to pay the full amount, which was almost double what I paid when Leigh was at the hospital. The manager told me that there was a difference in the rate reduction calculation for patients in what is called chronic or complex care and patients in long-term care. She admitted that it was something that even their own staff would likely be unaware of. I felt like the victim of some cruel bait and switch. Trying not to panic, I wondered how I was going to afford Leigh's accommodation and continue paying our mortgage along with everything else. Most nursing home residents are over the age of sixty-five with no dependents, but Leigh didn't fit that profile. He still had a wife and a child in school, trying their best to live normal lives in the middle of an abnormal situation. What a "sorry about your luck" kick in the gut. For a while I tried to fight it, starting an online petition and appealing to the government, but after more than one roadblock, I resigned myself to considering my options, from selling our house to cutting back on food.

Leigh had been with his new room mate, Joe, for about two months before I decided that I would have to ask that he be moved again. Leigh was upset because of all the noise that Joe made throughout the night, and despite wearing earplugs with his headphones over top, Leigh wasn't able to sleep. When he had another seizure, I thought the lack of sleep was a contributing factor. Again I was told that there were no other beds available. Eventually, Joe was accusing Leigh of stealing personal items like toothpaste. He even put me on the defensive one day, and I gave him the tube I had just purchased for Leigh. Each of them had their own storage cart in the bathroom, and I knew that Leigh needed assistance every day with hygiene, so I was certain it wasn't true that he was taking anything. Then one day we came in to find out from the social worker that Joe had threatened to kill Leigh. Immediately, I thought that the whole Charlie fiasco was happening all over again, but I was assured by the social worker that they were on top of it. They had advised Joe's family so that they could speak to him and they were assigning extra staff to monitor. Shortly thereafter, we found the bed beside Leigh was empty; Joe had been taken somewhere else. I wasn't sure where, but it didn't matter. Through the ongoing turmoil, God was waiting for me to let go. Even though I was praying, I was still relying on myself too much because that's what I had always done. As my own strength was being drained, I felt myself surrendering. God kept showing up, as I was leaving it with Him. I was finally finding some peace within the circumstance and within myself.

At the beginning, I was exasperated by small problems like Leigh's labelled clothes going missing or clothes that didn't belong to him showing up in his closet. I gave up complaining to the nursing staff because, ultimately, they weren't the ones responsible, and it was clear they were short on resources as it was. Besides, I don't think they appreciated my tone. As it is with much of the world, it came down to money. The home contracted out the work as cheaply as possible and that was that. Besides, I had bigger problems to deal with, so it just became something I put up with. Over time, I began to appreciate how caring and hard working most of the staff were.

The impact that Leigh was having on people, from the early days in the big city to his time at the rehab hospital, was evident. The more time he spent with people, from staff to patients to residents, the more you could see how he just radiated a light that drew people in. The pattern repeated itself at the Hen House. For a man with a vocabulary of little more than half a dozen words, it was remarkable how many people knew who he was and showed genuine affection for him. Brienne and I would come in to take Leigh home for a visit, and people would be greeting him and high-fiving him. The social worker told us that he was always trying to help others.

Even so, Leigh's magnetism and naïve innocence got him into trouble at times. There was a ninety-eight-year-old woman, Muriel, who developed an infatuation with him. The staff thought it was pretty funny, and for me, there was an awkward amusement. I definitely sensed a hostility from her whenever I came in and Leigh was trying to show me, by pointing at his wedding band, that he was making it clear that he was married. But there was a time or two that he expressed a desire for me to go talk to her and stake my claim so to speak. My feelings changed from amusement to embarrassment. There was no way I was going to do that, and I quickly changed the subject as I pushed his wheelchair towards the exit on our way to take Leigh home for a visit. I did bring it to the attention of the social worker and the staff was instructed to keep an eye on the situation and redirect Muriel if Leigh was clearly annoyed by her attention. Even though Leigh was expressing a desire to be distanced from Muriel, the social worker told me that he would park his wheelchair beside hers in the common area, and when he was given the option to change tables in the dining room to be away from her, he chose to stay. Maybe he just wanted to test me. I knew it disappointed him that I hardly ever kissed him, but I just couldn't. And, somewhere along the line, I had slipped off my wedding ring and put it in my purse. What was true before Leigh's transplant and stroke was still true now—I loved him, but not really like a wife loves a husband. Both of us had gone through a cataclysmic change, leaving our relationship as something not easily defined.

The Hen House was a place I tolerated; it wasn't a place I wanted to spend my time. The smells and the sounds of people begging for help were a grim reminder of aging, death and loneliness. Whenever I went there, either alone or with my daughter, I just wanted to take care of my business and run. Every time we were there, we felt people staring at us. Maybe it was because we appeared younger than most of the visitors. In fact, more than once, if a person didn't know who I was, they would mistake me for Leigh's daughter. Everything that had happened to Leigh had aged him considerably, and part of me wanted to escape from everything—including him sometimes—because the reality of it was almost more than I could bear.

Chapter Seven
Counterfeit Love

As time went on, I wondered if Leigh's family would keep up with the visits to see him at the Hen House. Surprisingly, his father appeared to be coming regularly—almost every Friday—but Cate was coming only once in a blue moon. I knew this because I would ask Leigh whether he had seen one or the other and, even though his memory would come and go, he could often give me a solid yes or no. Nonetheless, Leigh just lived in the moment, so the concern about who was coming and how often was more mine than his. He was more concerned with getting out of that place whenever he could.

The first summer that Leigh was at the Hen House, we were invited to attend the wedding of Cate's daughter. It was a beautiful afternoon in a park like setting, with the ceremony taking place outdoors. Scott and Kristine came as well, graciously helping me with Leigh so that both of us could relax and enjoy. Even Peter's wife, Tanya, came for the wedding; it was the first time in over a decade because it was no secret that she despised Willie. As we were making the rounds and saying our goodbyes, I had a short conversation with Cate in which she shocked me by saying that she had resented spending her Monday afternoons looking after Leigh when I had been caring for him at home. Then, as I was about to get in the car, Tanya said I could call anytime, and I jokingly replied, "As long as Peter doesn't screen the calls." I surprised myself when I said it. I thought I had gotten over it, but the pain of rejection burns like acid. Although it was nice to be out together and Leigh seemed to enjoy himself, I was left with mixed feelings at the end, mostly bad.

Only two days after the wedding, Leigh was hospitalized with pneumonia. Brienne and I were caught up in another whirlwind of worry, balancing school and work and visits to the hospital. After the end of the first week, I was certain that Willie knew about Leigh being in hospital because the Hen House would have told him when he went for his Friday visit. I called Willie and put him on the spot by boldly asking him if he was going to see his son; it caught him off guard. He sputtered and stumbled a bit to come up with a flimsy excuse.

Leigh was seriously ill; the doctors debated on whether to operate and open up his windpipe. My prayers were answered, and things turned around after almost three weeks in hospital. It was Leigh's birthday, and the day was beautiful and sunny when I brought him back to our house. He sat in his wheelchair out on the deck with his foot propped up on the railing, wearing his red baseball cap and the blue sling to hold his right arm. Out there, peace and freedom beckoned through the intermittent screech of a red tailed hawk and the rustling leaves from the trees in the nearby forest, unlike the constant symphony of torment at the Hen House. We had never had the money to build a deck at the back of the house but after placing Leigh in the nursing home, I decided to cash out more retirement savings to build it. Whenever Leigh was home, he loved to spend time out there.

I let Leigh's family back into my life, mainly for Leigh, but also as an unspoken gesture of my willingness to forgive. Lord knows I wanted to, for my own sake. And, I believed that God was using this tragedy and all the broken pieces leading up to it to rebuild me somehow, although it was difficult to envision how this could be the way—for old wounds to be re-opened while I was still trying to deal with the present. I recalled the prayer I had prayed years earlier, down on my knees in my closet, before Leigh's transplant and stroke—for truths to be revealed, for justice to be done and for the lost years to be regained.

The fact that no one had acknowledged any wrongdoing, left me believing there was no hope for any good relationship with them. It echoed what had happened with my own family and I had learned that offering up forgiveness in the face of denial was foolish. If they didn't see anything wrong with their behaviour and I just went along with them in pretending that it was fine, I would be enabling them to continue the mistreatment and hurting myself in the process.

I knew what it was like to have a mentally ill parent cause a covert, yet tsunami-level, destruction to other family members—the kind that carries hate and bitterness forward. Leigh, Cate and Peter weren't able to acknowledge what I could see—that they were afraid of their father. Yet, on the surface, they all gave the appearance of being well-adjusted, confident and self-assured. At least they had some kind of relationship with each other. But, for me, even though it wasn't what I would have chosen, I had no relationship with my siblings. When my father died, you could say that my entire family died as far as I was concerned. My efforts for a relationship with my mother, brother and sister were met with disdain, and eventually I had to face the truth that the only thing I could get out of a relationship with them was pain, leaving me no choice but to let them go.

In conversations I'd had with Cate since Leigh had his stroke, I was beginning to understand her attitude towards her brother had a lot to do with unresolved anger. She felt that Leigh showed a lack of concern for their mother when she was dealing with her own long-term illness. Nonetheless, I knew better than almost anyone that Leigh was too caught up in his own struggles to really see much beyond himself. It wasn't that he didn't love; he just didn't know how to love. The man he looked up to all his life set an example of putting self first, the opposite of love. What Leigh's family wasn't acknowledging was the fact that Leigh had endured increasingly serious health issues, with all the ramifications on his life, since he was a kid. He had denied or made light of his challenges by either suppressing or not dealing appropriately with his emotions, afraid to admit to weakness, because of the environment his father created. Leigh's bond with his family was unbalanced and unhealthy to the point of betraying the one person who had stood by him.

I came to recognize that Willie had all the characteristics of someone with narcissistic personality disorder. In researching the psychology of people under the influence of someone with this disorder, I found that there is a documented pattern of behaviour similar to that of a battered woman in a domestic abuse situation. It's called the trauma bond. To people who have never experienced it or not had reason to know about it, the behaviour appears to be irrational. In reality, it's a primal defence mechanism used to survive. A person who is held hostage by another, whether it be physically or psychologically, can develop feelings that appear to be love. They will defend their abuser, even though they are under a real or perceived threat by that person. It can be a psychological threat like a threat to a person's identity or a person's soul. In the case of children under the influence of a narcissistic father, they have no idea that they are victims. They're just trying to exist in an atmosphere where they're doused with intermittent kindness while also having their self-esteem gutted.

Not quite a month after Leigh was out of hospital and we were back in our usual routine, Cate called Brienne with an invitation to go out for Willie's birthday. The invitation was worded in such a way that it didn't specifically leave me out but didn't specify that I was welcome either. It was Cate extending the invitation, but I could hear Willie behind it. Immediately, it triggered a negative emotional response from me because, in my mind, I was taken back to the years in exile before Leigh's stroke. I made it clear that I wasn't going to go. Leigh, however, was excited about it, and he also wanted me to go. The pleading in his tone and his eyes tugged at my heart, but I just couldn't subject myself to that. I told myself that it didn't matter anyway because it made no sense for me to celebrate the man's birthday. But I was determined not to allow Willie to think he had gotten to me, and I wanted Leigh to enjoy himself. The evening came and I went after work to get Leigh from the nursing home, telling Willie he was welcome to come and pick him up. When Willie came, he barely acknowledged me, but I carried on with my "kill 'em with kindness" demeanour; I even gave him a birthday card. Maybe I was being paranoid, I thought. After everything I had done for his son, I didn't want to believe that Willie would go back to the passive agressive bullying.

I was in a spiritual battle against darkness and even though I knew in my heart that God was with me, it was difficult not to think that we were living through our own purgatory. Just like time no longer had any meaning for Leigh, it no longer had the same meaning for me. The world had gone on without me and I couldn't be part of it, no matter how hard I tried. The lack of any intensive therapy in the nursing home meant that the progress Leigh had made in trying to walk was all regressing, and the hope for Leigh ever coming home again was gone for me. I decided to stop bringing Leigh home for overnight visits on the weekends. Eventually, I was only bringing him home on Sunday afternoons for a few hours and then taking him back to the Hen House after dinner. In spite of myself and my attempt to create distance, those afternoons we spent together as a family grounded me somehow, like being wrapped up in a warm and familiar blanket; when it was time for him to go back, there was a sombre acceptance. The rest of the time, I was like a crystallized tree after an ice storm—frozen in time, weighed down and growing cold.

Scott and Erik were seeing Leigh regularly; for this I was grateful. Scott was also caring enough to call or check on me and we would swap stories or give each other updates on Leigh. As much I tried restraining myself, I couldn't resist the compulsion to make references here and there to the problem with Willie and the rest of the family. As compassionate as Scott generally was, I knew he still didn't get it and it bothered me. Scott was just trying to be Switzerland, trying not to take any sides. His main concern was Leigh and I couldn't fault him for that. He didn't understand the extent to which I had sacrificed myself for Leigh, the extent to which I had been attacked for doing so and how I was silently drowning in a place where I had no voice.

It was mid-summer roughly a year after Leigh moved to the Hen House, and on one of those evening phone conversations with Scott, the discussion took a turn. I felt that he wasn't really hearing me, so I started raising my voice and interrupting him. In doing so, I hit a nerve and he unleashed on me. He was standing firm with his childhood vision of Willie being the fun dad, of the great times that he had along with Leigh and the others in their group of friends. In previous conversations, I had tried to make him understand how difficult my own childhood was but, because he was so angry, he made a remark: "It couldn't be as bad as you say it was." I hung up on him. He called back in a fury and as far as I was concerned, he had crossed a line. In looking back, I could see the tension between us had been building but in that one conversation, our friendship was over.

After the argument with Scott, I was crushed. This person, who I knew had been a god-send through one of the worst times in my life, had turned on me. What did that say about me? When I told Brienne about it the following day, I was sobbing. A few days later, I had a panic attack. The next morning I felt weak and I stepped on the scale. It seemed I had lost several pounds overnight, and I told Brienne that she would have to drive me to the hospital. She was a bundle of nerves herself because neither of us knew what was wrong with me.

At the hospital, after all the preliminary questioning, I sensed skepticism from the doctor. I couldn't take another person not believing me. I blurted out something about our current circumstances, then I said, "The last place I want to be is in a hospital, and I wouldn't be in one without a good reason. Maybe I haven't been taking the best care of myself, but I've had a lot to deal with. I'm asking you to run some tests so that I know for sure there is nothing wrong. I can't afford to not be okay; I have to be here on this earth for her." And I looked over at Brienne. After that, the doctor ordered some blood tests, which showed I was anaemic and dehydrated, but there was nothing to indicate anything more serious. When we left the hospital, I was a bit embarrassed, but the relief I felt was greater.

I was too hurt to talk about the falling out with Scott. I went over it and over it in my mind, finally accepting that he didn't understand and there wasn't anything I could do. Intuition told me that I needed to be still and stop trying to do what only God could do. I knew the truth and so did God, and that would have to be enough. I was also aware that Brienne was in a very awkward position because Scott and Kristine had been so wonderful to us both. Kristine had recommended Brienne for a summer job where she worked, and she would often give Brienne a ride home. Neither Kristine nor Brienne could do much about it, and the cold war stretched into months between Scott and me.

The routine with Leigh continued, and I found myself on a kind of detached autopilot—like my body was moving, but my head was somewhere else. Now that all the crises had subsided, I was filled with doubts. The certainty that I was doing what God wanted me to do in looking after Leigh was shaken by thoughts that this was punishment for marrying him to begin with. Then, I was condemning myself for being such a martyr trying to show everyone what a great person I was in sacrificing myself.

We thought that Leigh was past trying to run away from the nursing home, but he escaped again during the summer of 2016. I wasn't as sympathetic as I had been in the past and my first reaction was agitation when I found him outside the house. Immediately, I told him that I was going to take him right back, but it was obvious he was upset, and my reaction upset him that much more. Brienne was watching, not knowing what to say. Something inside me changed, and I dropped my anger, offering instead to bring him inside for something to eat and to stay a while. Once we were inside, I started to question him as to what happened, but that just led to more frustration on both sides. He then made a gesture with his left arm and hand like someone jumping off a diving board, along with a half-whistling sound. Both Brienne and I knew what he was saying and the room was silent; I was fighting back tears. There was a storm water pond within walking distance of our house, and he was indicating that he wanted to drown himself.

After I collected myself, I told him that I understood why he felt that way. Never could I have envisioned myself enduring what he had with such strength and resilience, and I told him so. "There are so many people who love you. How do you think Brienne and I would feel if you did that? You couldn't do that to us. And, much as you hate it at the Hen House, there are people there that care about you." When we took Leigh back that evening, he appeared resigned to it. We loved him, and he knew it; we told him every single time that we left him in that place.

Summer passed. It was fall and Brienne's nineteenth birthday was coming up. Again, Cate was being used as a pawn in Willie's malicious game of pretending I didn't exist. Leigh and Brienne were invited to go out to dinner, in honour of Brienne's birthday, with Willie, Cate, her daughter and new son-in-law. Brienne and Leigh were my entire world, and I had devoted myself to them both. Our only daughter was crossing over from adolescence to young adulthood, through some of the worst years anyone could ever experience. Yet, I wasn't fit to be part of her birthday celebration. How could anyone think this was right? There was no mistaking it now. The war against me was evident.

As the birthday dinner approached, I tried my best to push it out of my mind and not let it get to me. I didn't want to be angry at Leigh or Brienne, but, at the same time, I was insulted that they so passively went along with it. Then, when Brienne and I went to the Hen House one Sunday to visit Leigh, the subject of her birthday came up again. Yes, I knew that Leigh couldn't speak but it felt like the past all over again, when he wouldn't stand up for me. I was so upset that I got up and started walking out, feeling angry and guilty at the same time. I was outside and headed for the car when I turned around to see Brienne standing beside Leigh in his wheelchair. He appeared so bewildered that I could hardly stand to look. Brienne said goodbye to him and followed me to the car. The two of us sat in silence as I drove us to the mall.

The position I was being put in was impossible and I couldn't stand it. Sitting down on the first empty bench I found in the middle of the mall, I called Cate from my cell phone. I hadn't heard from her since her daughter's wedding which had been months ago. Even though I had always been a bit intimidated by Cate because she appeared so confident and extroverted, I was provoked enough to toss all of my self-doubt aside. Speaking loudly because of the noise around me, the discussion became heated and soon I was yelling. People were beginning to stare, but I didn't care. Brienne looked on in embarrassment.

"Do you think it's right that I'm not invited to my own daughter's birthday dinner?"

Cate answered as if she was speaking for the entire family.

"We didn't think you wanted anything to do with us," she said.

The inference was that I had no right to be angry. Willie didn't even have to be present to pull the strings of his children. He was adept at dodging responsibility for his behaviour by playing the victim.

I confronted Cate about her comment at the wedding, about resenting the Monday afternoons with Leigh. At first she vehemently denied saying it, but when I wasn't backing down, she made an excuse that centred around her mother. I recognized the self-pity in the excuses, maybe because God was helping me to see the same thing in myself. I knew her life hadn't been easy, but mine hadn't been either. At one point, I told her that it wasn't a contest. Then I brought up the infrequent visits to the nursing home and she seemed surprised that I was aware. When she said the reason for not visiting the home was because she was depressed, anger broke through my restraint.

"You're depressed?! I sacrificed myself, putting Leigh and Brienne ahead of my own feelings." As the conversation continued, her attitude shifted from confrontation to one that was paying more attention to what I was saying. I told her how deeply hurt I was, all those years ago, because no one reached out to me after Hattie verbally attacked me, letting Willie use her as a weapon against me because he "didn't like my tone." I was the one who was blamed.

Cate agreed that her father was not a good man, but she also started to say that Leigh was like her father in a lot of ways. "Partly," I said. "Leading up to the second transplant and after he lost his driver's license, his anger was frightening at times. But there's a big difference between the two. Leigh has a good heart; the old man has a heart of stone." Cate agreed and she said that she tried to have as little to do with her father as possible, even though they lived on the same street. By the end of the conversation, I felt like a weight was being lifted as truth was starting to shine like a light through a crack in the door. I still wasn't invited to the birthday dinner but perhaps it was best that way. I had no energy for playing Willie's games or for a confrontation. Cate and I agreed that we would go out separately, with our daughters, to celebrate Brienne's birthday.

I picked up the phone one December evening and it was Scott. It had been about six months since we had last spoken, and I truly thought I might never speak to him again. He apologized. The words were like a flood of living water through my soul. Finally, someone who was important to me, someone who had hurt me, saw me as a person worthy of an apology. During the time of silence between us, I had some revelations of my own. I said, "There is no way you could really understand what I had been through, and I was wrong to expect that. I know that your memories are real, that you had good times with Leigh and his family when you were growing up, and those good times included Willie. But there were things beneath the surface and behind closed doors that no one knew."

I knew that it was much more difficult for people to acknowledge and understand emotional and psychological abuse—how it can destroy a person's soul, how it can set up a person for failure in almost every area of their life. In my own experience, it's more devastating than physical abuse. Physical abuse is much easier to identify, it's more black and white, and people have no difficulty in agreeing that it's wrong and that the person subjected to it is a victim. Emotional abuse is more subtle; it's crafty, nasty and sneaky. It's like a toxin that is designed to release itself in a slow and steady stream, saturating the roots of any living thing, depriving it of what it needs to thrive. If the victim is strong enough or self-aware enough to try to speak up, often people dismiss it or minimize it or, in the extreme, blame the victim. It's much easier for the person inflicting the damage to continue their behaviour, undetected and unchallenged.

I was thankful that we could continue the new tradition we started at the rehab hospital of "the best worst Christmas ever," bringing Leigh to share a meal with Scott and Kristine, their friends and family. We were all welcome there; we could all laugh and be ourselves.

Then, I fortified myself because I was trying again to make an effort with Leigh's family. I knew that Peter had driven into town for a few days, so I invited Cate and Peter to come over to our house for tea. Cate asked about Willie, and I hesitated before saying that he could come too. I brought Leigh home for the occasion, and it was all very civil until Willie asked an odd question about the stair lift. What he didn't know was that I had sold the lift months ago when I stopped bringing Leigh home for overnight stays. When he heard that I no longer had the lift, there was silence and a look in his eyes that was frightening. That man would have danced if it had been me who was in the nursing home instead of his son. I knew that Willie had been telling Leigh that he was going to walk again, even though by now it was clear that he wouldn't. Willie was saying that Leigh should be at home again, but when Cate asked him who was going to look after him, Willie said, "the house will."

Chapter Eight
Peace

The soul no longer bound
To what couldn't be maintained
The missiles launched against
No longer a concern
And veils that covered truths
Have all been stripped away

We were heading into the new year but I was more weary than hopeful. It had now been a little over three years since the life we had known evaporated, leaving us in a mourning that never seemed to end. I was leaning heavily on my faith for the strength to keep going, praying every day before I left the house and hiding favourite scriptures in my heart and mind.

Every year, there was a care conference at the Hen House where I would meet with the doctor and nurse coordinator to discuss Leigh. I was committed to all Leigh-related appointments and duties, but I wasn't pouring myself out the way I had been. The anecdotes about Leigh that came to me from time to time were like nudges to help me get back into focus. The doctor told me how, more than once, she had gone into Leigh's room to check on him and knocked over his urinal which sat on the arm of his wheelchair by the bed. Urine splashed all over her and she was amazed that Leigh would remember every time he saw her, pointing at the urinal and laughing.

On a Sunday, when Leigh was at home with us, the phone rang.

My heart started to race when I saw my mother's name on the call display, and I paused before yelling out for Brienne to pick it up. Whatever my mother was asking, Brienne was giving tentative and polite one-word answers. The brief small talk about weather and school surrounded the real reason for her call—morbid curiosity. In what Brienne described as a feeble and shaky voice that sounded like it could be from the grave, she blatantly asked, "Is your dad dead yet?" Then, towards the end of the call, she said to Brienne, "Don't tell anyone—I'm not supposed to be calling." Knowing she was mentally ill didn't stop me from being upset by what she said. Soon after, I realized that it was the Christmas card I sent her that must have prompted her to call. It had been signed with only my name and Brienne's; I didn't sign Leigh's name as I had in the past. I wondered if my mother really did want to reach out to me and perhaps my brother was preventing it. But, then again, having him control everything seemed to be the way she wanted it. After my father passed away, the two of them made it painfully obvious that I wasn't welcome in their lives. There was no rationality behind it, but greed was part of it. The other part was a jealousy I could never understand. I wasn't welcome in the house or on the land that had been my father's legacy where he had always gladly accepted me when he was alive.

A week or two went by and I was still wondering about my mother, so I decided to power up over my fear and make the call. She answered the phone and at first she sounded pleased to hear from me. And maybe it would have been a pleasant conversation if I had stayed within the boundaries of small talk. But I was determined not to be lulled into the same lie I had been telling myself all of my life— everything is okay and my mother really does love me after all. Speaking truth to her was always risky. She would lash out and what she would say didn't have to make sense, it just needed to hurt. When she asked how I was, I decided against the usual pat answer.

"I'm disappointed in you, Troy and Karen."

She was caught off guard.

"I was there for you when Dad died," I said abruptly.

She echoed the phrase "there for you" back to me in confusion.

"You waited until he died, and then you went out to change your will to cut me out and give everything to your favourite—Troy. You knew that Dad would not have approved."

I had been there for both of my parents until the last moments of my father's life but she wasn't interested in my support after the estate was settled. When I tried to make plans to see her, she made up excuses. I believed it was because she didn't want to upset my brother. Shortly after my father passed away, she made me feel guilty for being a bit late for an appointment at the lawyer's office. My father made me a co-executor of his estate along with my mother and brother. It took a long time for the truth to sink in—that my mother wasn't interested in me at all or the love I tried to give. All she wanted was my signature on the documents that would transfer over all of my father's investments and assets. And then from her, to my brother's hands, cutting me out of any future inheritance.

"Did you know that Leigh is in a nursing home, in a wheelchair, that he can't walk or talk or take care of himself? And you don't care! You don't give a damn! I screamed. He was always kind to you, and you don't give a damn!" Her response were words spoken as though to curse me: "You're at the end of your line," and she laughed. I was so overwrought by that time, I was shaking.

"I don't know why I bothered! You're just a horrible, hateful person!" I yelled into the phone and hung up. For all I knew, that would be the last conversation I would ever have with her.

My heart would jump every time I saw the Hen House show up on my call display because it usually meant there was a problem. I lost count of the calls throughout the two years Leigh had been there. For a long time, I would get up in the middle of the night, or whenever it was, to be there with him and speak for him. Having to deal with work and these unexpected crises at all hours was wearing on me, so I tried gauging the severity of the problem before deciding whether to go to the hospital or not. If it was a fall and they found that there were no broken bones, they transported him back to the home. A trip like that would usually mean at least eight hours of waiting, and I knew the hospital would call me if I was needed.

Then, one evening in June, I had one of those calls from the Hen House. It wasn't clear what was wrong, but Leigh was having pains in his stomach or abdomen, and he indicated that he thought he should go to the hospital, so they sent him by ambulance. I didn't think it sounded that serious and I had work the next morning, so my plan was to check in at the nursing home before going to work. My cell phone rang in the middle of the night. It was a doctor asking me to come to the hospital to answer some questions. Even then I hesitated. At that moment, I felt deeply ashamed. Over the last few years, I had fallen so far from where I had been—from being full of purpose in knowing this is what God wanted me to do to feeling deeply resentful of the burden and the cost.

Brienne found me getting ready to head out the door when she arrived home from her midnight shift so she came with me. When we arrived, Leigh was still in the Emergency Department, and a doctor told me that there were a couple of problems.

"The pain that your husband is having is because of a hernia. The good news is that we managed to push it back in place." I was relieved. But that wasn't the end.

"The CT scan has shown that there's something obstructing his bowel. We need your consent for surgery." We were standing near Leigh's bed and I said to the doctor, "Yes, go ahead and operate."

When we all stepped outside of Leigh's cubicle, the doctor's demeanour was grim as he explained.

"It isn't that straight forward. In fact, it's a very risky surgery. We believe that the obstruction is most likely a tumour. With all of your husband's health complications, he would undoubtedly end up in ICU, and it would not likely be a good outcome." Brienne and I were stunned and I had to sit down. The choice would need to be made soon. Leigh was going to be admitted and further consultation would be done by more specialists, so for the time being, Brienne and I kept quiet, partly from shock and partly because we didn't want to upset Leigh. We kissed him goodbye, telling him we would be back later, and we went home.

Later that evening, I smiled when Scott told me about his visit with Leigh at the hospital. He and Erik had gone there after finding Leigh wasn't at the Hen House. While they were with him, Leigh needed a urinal. None of the hospital staff were paying attention so Leigh put his hand up as if to say, "Wait guys, this is how it's done," and then he started making a big racket, yowling and clamouring with "Leigh-speak". Someone was there in under thirty seconds. That was classic Leigh.

After what felt like an eternity, Leigh was out of the Emergency Department and into a private room. I was called back to the hospital to talk to a surgeon and a doctor about surgery. Discussions took place in Leigh's room. It was understood that Leigh wasn't completely competent, but, at the same time, he was cognizant enough to be part of any decision. We were told that the surgery was extremely risky; it was a long shot that he would even survive it. Leigh was at a higher risk for cancer because he was on immunosuppressant drugs. Because of that, they believed that the obstruction was a tumour, but they didn't know if it was benign or cancerous. What I wasn't prepared to hear was that Leigh would certainly die if he didn't have the operation. Currently, ninety-five percent of his colon was blocked. The decision to go ahead needed to be made soon.

At first, when I asked Leigh if he wanted the surgery, he shook his head and waved his hand from side to side as an emphatic no. When the doctor asked him again directly, Leigh looked at me and I said it was his decision. Leigh suddenly changed his mind and indicated yes. The doctors left the room to schedule it. When they left, Leigh was looking at me as he said "OK?"

"Why did you say yes? Is it because you're scared?" I asked Leigh. He started to cry.

"I understand" I said, with tears rolling down my cheeks. "But you know you're not happy as it is now. Even if you made it through the surgery, you would end up in bad shape in intensive care, and if the tumour was cancerous, then you wouldn't survive the chemotherapy. Do you still want to go through with it?"

"No," he said.

Suddenly I had an impulse to pull out the folded piece of paper I had carried in my purse for a while. It was the salvation prayer.

"Okay, you're going to listen. For everything that you have gone through here on this earth, you are not going to miss out on what is being offered in what I say next." I read the prayer out loud, and then I said to Leigh, "Do you accept it?"

As he wept, he nodded and said yes. I was overjoyed. Never in a million years would I have expected such a thing. God knew how much it had always bothered me that Leigh didn't believe, and He knew how much it hurt me to think that all his suffering would be in vain. There was no doubt in my mind that I had just witnessed the grace and power of the Holy Spirit. The gift was just as much for me as it was for Leigh.

I left the room and looked for one of the doctors we had spoken with. When I found him, I told him that Leigh had changed his mind about the surgery, and I wanted him to come back into the room to hear it from Leigh. When the doctor asked him again, Leigh was settled with a no.

I went to work the following day, rushing home at lunch because I had a conference call with various medical professionals, the doctors who had been on Leigh's case and the head nurse at the Hen House. This was to ensure everyone was on the same page regarding Leigh's care and to provide me the opportunity to ask questions. The main question on my mind was how much time he had? The answer was vague. It could be three months, it could be less if he didn't have any food. Or, it could be six months. They couldn't say. The diet plan was for soft foods only. Leigh was going to be discharged and transported back to the Hen House that afternoon. I had been keeping Leigh's sister up to date, and she decided she would go see her brother as soon as he got back to the nursing home. While I was at work, I heard my cell phone buzz. Cate had been waiting for an hour and Leigh hadn't shown up. What now, I thought. I called the hospital and found out that they had decided to keep Leigh in hospital because when they tested his INR, which is a measure of blood clotting, it was too high. He had been on warfarin, an anticoagulant, since the stroke, but now, given the current situation, he wasn't going to be on it any longer. They needed to reverse the high INR quickly. When I arrived at the hospital later that day, the nurses had called the doctor to come back to the hospital. Brienne and I sat in the room feeling helpless. They had given Leigh a blood transfusion, but now he was spiking a fever. At that point, it was apparent that we were in for a long night. And based on Leigh's condition, it didn't appear he would be leaving the hospital anytime soon. As the night went on, Leigh's fever finally broke and he seemed a bit better. I subscribed to the TV service for the room, but when I turned it on, only one channel was available. Obviously, it wasn't working. There we were—the three of us intently watching someone make Chicken Marsala.

"Are you sure this doesn't bother you? A show about food and now you can't eat solid food?" I asked looking over at Leigh. It was like a cruel joke, but one that didn't seem to phase him at all.

The following day, Leigh was stable enough to be transported back to the Hen House. I considered finding Leigh a better place for his end of life care, but he wanted to stay there because it was familiar and the staff knew him. They all appeared to know that he had come back with a death sentence. I pushed Leigh's wheelchair in and around the corner to the nurse's station, and they were all welcoming him back, some with high fives. I was putting on a smile, but they knew better. Some of them said, "Sorry Lori," but I didn't really want to talk about it. His one friend there, Judy, waved me over and asked how Leigh was. It had not sunk in for me yet, so I just told her in a matter-of-fact way as I watched the shock and empathy transform her expression.

The home was keeping Leigh to a mostly liquid diet because of the bowel obstruction, but it was obvious that he wanted solid food. He would go to the dining room at meal time and get angry that he couldn't eat what he wanted. I asked if he could have ice cream or yogurt because he was starving with what they were giving him. Part of me thought, what does it matter if they give him what he wants at this point? So, Brienne and I smuggled in a hamburger one night and Leigh was in heaven. It boosted his spirits and it didn't seem to do much harm, so every once in a while, we would bring something in— a slice of pizza or a sub sandwich. Then, Scott and Erik started doing the same thing. However, over time I started to see the effects: it was greater suffering for Leigh when he tried to go to the bathroom. Sometimes he was so weak, they had to use the patient lift to take him off the toilet and put him into bed. So, the contraband food was cut back.

Mike started to visit Leigh frequently, bringing him a drink or something to eat. He would often write to tell me about the visit: *I brought Leigh an iced cappuccino with a shot of espresso this afternoon and we had a nice walk around the neighbourhood. When I mentioned that I was eager to get to a restroom Leigh was gracious enough to hold out his empty coffee cup to assist in my moment of need. Hysterical! What an incredible sense of humour.*

I was in awe of Leigh's courage, of how he appeared to accept his place in time even though he was a lot weaker, in pain and often nauseated. Later I realized that Leigh was hiding a lot of his emotion from me. After another one of Mike's visits, he wrote: *He sat in the restroom for about forty-five minutes, sobbing while I massaged his back. He eventually got back in his wheelchair, washed his hands and came with me to the parking lot to bid me farewell. I think he was having trouble urinating and his pain was so intense that the nurse decided to take his vitals. He clearly conveyed the bottled-up frustration (shaking his left hand with his fist clenched) and the word "Why" repeated a number of times through his period of weeping.*

It had been a couple of weeks, and Leigh wondered where his father was. He had visited once when Leigh was still in hospital, but not since he had returned to the Hen House. I respected Leigh's desire to see his father, but I would not deal with him any longer. Cate was reaching out more, and she was acting as the liaison when it came to Willie, so she told her father that Leigh wanted to see him.

Leigh's fifty-eighth birthday was coming up in a couple of weeks, and it didn't seem real to think that this would be the final one. One morning, as I was getting ready for the day, there was a thought that wouldn't leave me alone. The thought was for me to put my wedding ring back on. At first, I couldn't remember where I had placed it as I looked in my jewelry box, panicking for a moment when it wasn't there. I ran to find my purse, hoping it was in the little zippered pocket; my fingers were glad to touch the cool metal and slip it back on.

Cate invited me to come over to her house and talk, so I decided I should take her up on the offer. I hadn't been to her house in so many years, I had lost count. We talked about the work she had done on her house, the grooming business that she ran out of her basement and her two cats. After all of that kind of talk was over, it was time to sit down with a cup of tea and carefully open up about the things that had torn us all apart. Inevitably, we always came back to our common ground, which was the misery caused by her father. She said that she was afraid that he had gotten away with what he had done to her mother. I didn't hesitate at all when I said, "Well, I don't know if we will see it, but I know one thing for sure—that I've given it to God and justice will be done."

Leigh was losing weight rapidly and he was weaker, but he was almost always eager to get outside when someone came. I was still trying to bring Leigh home for a few hours on the weekends, as long as he had the strength, and his birthday was a beautiful sunny summer afternoon. There were walking trails near our house, and one of them led to an old abandoned apple orchard on the edge of protected woodland. Erik had given us an old electric wheelchair with a left-handed toggle switch so that Leigh could control it. That weekend, Leigh wanted to get in the chair and go sit near the trees for a while. It was a peaceful little oasis surrounded by swaying cedars, with the odd flash of yellow from a darting gold finch. Leigh smiled as he put his hand on his bald head, moving his hand over it as if to smooth out a full head of hair.

At the beginning of August, Scott called me to say that Erik had gone for a visit and found Leigh extremely upset. Apparently, Willie had been there just before Erik showed up, and Leigh was so furious, it took quite a while for Erik to calm him down. In fact, he had never seen Leigh so angry. Scott told me that the long and the short of it was that Leigh did not want his father to come back—ever. I was in shock because Leigh had blindly idolized that man, no matter what. The nursing home called to ask me what I thought. I told them I hadn't had a chance to speak to Leigh, but I supported his choice.

Leigh was in his room when I next came to visit; he was spending less time out in the public areas of the home. I eased into asking him about what happened.

"So, your father did something or said something to upset you?" I asked.

He pointed at the chair in the corner by the bed and yelled, "No, No, No."

"Was your father sitting there?" I said.

"Yeah," he said.

Then, he pointed at the curtain that was between the two beds. Usually the curtain wasn't pulled to divide them, but he was motioning with his arm and hand to show me that the curtain was pulled. I asked him if his father had done it and he nodded.

"What did he say?" I blurted out, but as soon as I said it, I knew Leigh couldn't answer. He pointed at me.

"He said something about me?" I asked.

He nodded and waved his hand from side to side as if to say, "sort of or partly."

"Was he saying things against me?" I said.

He was nodded and motioned his hand as if to say, "keep going." Intuition told me to ask if Cate and Hattie were included, so I did, and Leigh replied with an emphatic "Yeah!"

"So it was some anti-woman rant with me as the main target?"

Leigh, again, said an emphatic "Yeah." As he was telling me, it was apparent that he was still upset by it. Again, he pointed at the chair to show how he shut down his father with one simple word—

No. God's strength was made perfect in Leigh's weakness. Willie got up from the chair in the corner of the room and walked out without another word. Evil was turned on its head that day.

Tears started to come, and I threw my arms around Leigh because he had finally done it; seated in his wheelchair, he had stood up for himself and for me!

"I'm so proud of you; I can hardly believe it. Thank you. I'm just sorry that you had to go through that." I asked him if he might want to see his father at some point later and he said no. I asked him what he thought about our daughter still seeing or talking to her grandfather, and he also said no.

It was astounding. For well over a decade I had tried to get my husband to understand how toxic his father was. It had been the thing that ultimately destroyed my trust in him. I had no reason to think that Leigh would ever see the truth, especially given his current condition. Leigh sat by the window in his wheelchair and I sat on the edge of his bed. Finally, even though we were physically separated, we had been reunited or reconciled in ways that could not be seen. We talked, and when I say "we" I mean that he nodded and agreed, about how we had been robbed of so many years in our marriage. It was shared sorrow over time and love lost. But, at the same time, it was recognition of a love between us that had been given back.

Cate was dreading telling her father that he had been banned from the nursing home so she asked Peter to make the seven-hour drive, so they could tell him together. Cate said that, after what happened between Leigh and her father, one of the neighbours on the street had seen Willie, and he confided that he screwed things up. But by the time Cate and Peter spoke to Willie, he had come up with a convoluted story. He claimed that he was trying to help his dying son come clean to me, implying that my husband had hidden some deep, dark, shameful secret. There was absolute ludicrous depravity in everything about it. Even if Leigh had something to come clean about, everyone knew he couldn't communicate. Willie wanted to plant an evil seed of doubt in my mind about my husband, attempting to steal what God had just given us. I didn't believe it, but even if Leigh had done something beyond what I already knew, I didn't care. I knew that Leigh loved me, and that was all that mattered.

I hadn't recognized right away the breadth of the miracles that had taken place. Over the following weeks and months, I had begun to see that Leigh's stand with his father hadn't only restored the trust that had been broken in our marriage, it had started to open eyes. Cate and Leigh were repairing their relationship, and the divide that had been between all of us was being bridged. She was coming to the nursing home more regularly. We would often sit together near Leigh's bed, lost in conversation as we kept him company. Cate thanked Leigh for what he did in standing up to their father because she didn't feel alone anymore. It gave her the courage to confront him about how he had treated their mother and lied about seeing another woman while Hattie was ill. I knew Cate was not a believer, but I was bursting with a need to tell her about my conviction that it was God who worked this out through my faith and my prayers for truth and justice. I knew without a doubt that what happened with Leigh and his father wasn't a random coincidence. How could anyone have guessed that Leigh, a dying man who could only speak a handful of words, would have been the instrument to reveal the truth and, with that, impart the freedom to speak it out loud without fear of others disbelieving? God uses the least likely to accomplish his purposes. The walls that had risen between the victims of Willie's narcissistic abuse were finally falling down.

One evening, as I was sitting with Leigh, a nurse came in to give him his morphine injection. For the first while, I noticed that the injections were very painful for him. This particular nurse was not one of the regulars, and when he asked Leigh a question, Leigh, with tears welling up, put his finger to his temple as if to shoot himself. Then he just started yelling "Why?" over and over. The nurse just stood there, not knowing how to respond. After the nurse gave Leigh the injection and left the room, I could see that he was still distraught. I asked him if it would help for me to go home and grab the bible to read to him. I was surprised that he agreed because he never showed much interest in any book, let alone the bible. Maybe he agreed because it meant I would spend more time with him than I usually did. I did as I promised and the reading appeared to bring him comfort, so that by the time I left, he was peaceful.

However, Leigh wasn't letting go of the idea of ending his life, and he was expressing it to his sister and his friends. After one of Cate's visits, she contacted me asking if I would consider medically assisted death. This was something that had been allowed by law only about a year prior. I heard Cate out because she was trying to speak on Leigh's behalf and over concern for his prolonged suffering. Instinctively and because of my belief, I was against it. I had been there for Leigh like no one else, and I hated what he was going through. Still, that made me more determined to have him hang in there. I was certain that this was a temporary state that would lead to *"a tremendous and eternal glory, much greater than the trouble."* (2 Corinthians 4:17) My intuition told me that invisible forces were trying to undo the salvation that Leigh had already accepted. Nevertheless, I made some enquiries as to the process in order to be fully informed and out of respect for what Leigh was trying to express. I discovered that it involved interviews with doctors outside of the nursing home. When I enquired with the Hen House head nurse, she corroborated the fact that it was a lengthy and thorough process. So, when Cate brought it up to me again while we were together with Leigh in his room, I told them both what I learned. I told Leigh that I didn't agree with a medically assisted death and if he wanted to end his own life sooner, he should just stop eating. When I spoke to the nurse on duty she made it clear that the home would not stop feeding him. So, I told Leigh that if that was what he wanted it was up to him to refuse to eat.

Scott called to talk one night soon after that; he was obviously upset. Then, he told me how he wept as Leigh begged him to put an end to everything by putting the pillow over his face.

"I know buddy, but I can't do it. It's against the law and Lori won't either; she's a godly woman." Scott had told him.

Leigh wept, "I know."

Summer evenings gave way to fall. I continued to go to work, come home, take a nap, grab something quick to eat and then take the fifteen-minute walk to the nursing home. For a long time, I had been feeling like a ghost, as if my head wasn't attached to my body. It didn't feel right to be walking down the street, past the happy homes, people laughing, playing and living life, on my way to the place where my husband was dying.

This year, just as in past years, around Brienne's birthday and the anniversary of my Dad's death, I went with Brienne to visit my father's grave. The cemetery was in a small town about a half-hour drive away, and we would combine the trip with a dinner in town. On the way, we stopped at a flower shop to buy a single rose, but they gave it to me for free when I told them it was for someone in the cemetery. We parked and walked over to his stone. I couldn't believe my eyes. My father had been gone for ten years, but the ground adjacent to the stone was freshly dug up. This was a plot that was meant for my mother to share when she passed, but I had come to the realization that my brother would not tell me if she had. I concluded that she must have died recently and, remembering my last conversation with her, I was left feeling unsettled. It was a Friday evening, so I spent the weekend upset, believing she was dead and that I hadn't been told. The following week, when I spoke to the cemetery caretaker, I found out that no one had been buried; the ground had settled and they had simply added topsoil! I laughed at the absurdity of it all, but I was relieved. That was the impetus for me to try again. This time, after praying to God for courage and more control over my emotions, I decided to call my mother again.

Her voice was almost other worldly.

"Hello?"

"Hello," I said back. She said hello again.

"Can you hear me?" I asked. She hung up. I re-dialled. She answered again.

"Can you hear me?" I asked again.

"Yes I can hear you."

"Do you know who this is?"

"No, I don't."

"It's Lori."

"I thought you went under."

"What do you mean?" I replied.

"The story was that you drowned in the water."

"Oh. Who said that?"

"I don't know. Too many people to keep track of," she replied.

I asked if she was home alone and she replied that she was. I inquired if she remembered our last conversation and she said that she did, but that she could not be held responsible for that.

"You didn't think I had a right to be upset?" I replied.

"Well…we're upset too."

"We?"

Of course, I knew she meant herself and my brother, but it irked me that she always referred to him in a way that suggested they were a couple. When I asked why they would be upset, she started talking about a roof that needed to be replaced.

"That's what bothers you? So, the fact that I was angry about you not…you know…caring about Leigh and me and what happened, you're not concerned about that at all?" I said.

"You are responsible for your own stuff."

Again, as lost as she was in her mind, there was no mistaking the message she had for me. She didn't care about my troubles, she didn't care about my anguish, she didn't care about my pain or her part in any of it. I was really having to hold myself back as it continued. "So it's okay for my brother to hate me then?" I said.

"I don't know that he hates you. He hates me. The only one that he doesn't hate is the cat. He takes good care of her."

"Well, it's pretty sad, you know; I'm your oldest daughter. I was there for you when Dad died and helped you as much as I could. And when I went through hell, you didn't bother to pick up the phone."

"Yeah, well, I have enough to deal with, diseases in my system, I don't need to worry about things that you can handle. Troy takes good care of me with my vegetables and all the stuff that goes with a good home."

"Right, but you're not responsible to care for anyone but Troy, is that right? As a mother, you don't think you have any obligation to love all your children, not just your favourite."

"There's no favourite."

"Oh, there always has been mother. You always doted on Troy."

"Well, at least we're not in the middle of a war. We can take time to listen to the ones that belong here."

"Right, so I never belonged and that's the way you all made me feel."

"I care as much as my body will let me."

"Well, I'm sure that you were much more together or well four or five years ago. In fact, I think it has been eight years since Leigh had his first transplant, but even then you couldn't wait to ditch me after Dad died."

"Oh I don't know, it's not worth it, think today and look to the future."

"Well, yeah, you're right but it's sad when a mother doesn't love her own daughter."

"Oh by cracky."

"Yeah, oh by cracky! It's easy for you to dismiss, I guess, because you don't have any feelings…can't force that."

"I have feelings for people who are genuine."

"Oh, and so are you saying I'm not genuine, is that what you're saying?!"

"That's the word that goes around this locality."

"Right, and when Dad died, you were afraid you didn't have enough money to live on, and who was it that offered you all that I had if you needed it?"

"I don't think—"

"It was me that offered it! But it just so happened that Troy told me that you had more than enough to live on!"

"He's got to think of it that way because every week there is a bill that comes in…if we don't then we could be like the neighbours…they were shot because they were not keeping up on the community. We happen to be the worst ones. They're giving us time to work our butt off. If we don't, we'll be on the firing squad. I'm not kidding. Some of them sleep with their so-called friends. But it isn't true because the government wants their money."

My mother was becoming more irrational, and for some reason it defused my anger; instead, I was feeling an awareness of just how incredibly tragic it all was—how lost she was. I asked about my sister. She had seen her maybe three years ago and had made her a quilt that she was pleased with but when I asked if they were on good terms she was non-committal. She said she was like any other person really, "take it with a grain of salt."

"She doesn't make friends. She just listens or curses," my mother declared. "She's a hard one to get across. She thinks of her own. I don't know how long, she'll be ready for the firing squad."

Then my mother told me about an incident where she had fallen out of bed while no one was home. Her heart had stopped, and she was almost dead. Someone must have found her because she started talking about being sent to hospital and being unconscious for a month. Then, she was transferred to the small-town hospital for another two weeks before going home. She talked about the nurses at the local hospital being kind. How ironic that the kindness of the nurses deserved a mention but my efforts to love her were not only unappreciated, they were unwanted. Rejection by a parent inflicts a kind of pain that can kill your spirit, even when you know that parent is broken. When I told her that Leigh was going to die soon, she said she wouldn't be surprised.

"Well, it's not because you've been keeping in touch, but okay," I said.

She made an excuse, saying that she didn't have my phone number and that she knew I was moving around. "I've been in the same place for eight years" and there was a pause before I continued.

"Well, I guess this conversation is better than the other one."

Then she started saying she was scared to go to the mail box because "the neighbours were shooting..." I asked if my brother forbid her to call me, and she admitted that he did. She was quick to say that it was only because they didn't have the phone number. Then I reminded her that she must have my phone number because she had called it in January.

"So did he tell you not to call?"

"It had nothing to do with you. He said that the calls that are coming in are utter nonsense, and we don't need to answer them."

"That's solicitors and people selling things—I haven't been calling you. Right?" I replied.

"Yes, that's right". Then she was talking about the answering service, which was her way of referring to an answering machine, as a way to screen calls.

There really wasn't anything else to say, and I could see it really didn't make a difference, so I just told her I was signing off. Oddly, she told me to have a good day.

"You too," I replied, followed by goodbye.

Immediately, a weight was lifted from me. In making it clear that she didn't care about me or couldn't care about me, my mother had given me the only thing she could. She had just released me from a bitterness that was rooted in the unfulfilled expectation of being loved by her. It wasn't because of me; it was because of her. My life and choices had been shaped because I believed the lies that I wasn't worthy of love. I hadn't even been aware of it. If that's how it was for me, it had to be that way for my brother and sister too. Self-loathing turns you into something that God never created you to be. All I had left was a deep sense of loss and sadness.

Who wouldn't expect their own mother to love them? Who would expect a mother to hide her disdain until she was so far gone that she just couldn't any more? The more I tried to hold on to the idea of the relationship, the way that it should be or should have been, the more harm I was doing to myself. That explained my pattern of choosing the wrong people: damaged people, people who needed to be fixed. Of course, I wasn't aware of it when I was living it. Hanging on to relationships where I did all the giving, as if I needed to prove my worth, was like a kind of self-mutilation. It was as deadly as any addiction. I could understand how Leigh subconsciously craved love from his father because the love of a parent should be a given. I could also understand what it is to be in a state of perpetual confusion because of the mixed signals coming from an unstable or abusive parent. Deep down you think that you're not good enough, and you blame yourself. Having that love becomes the carrot on a stick, forever sought after and forever out of reach. What it does to a person's soul is so profound that it sets one up for failure in all future intimate relationships, unless and until awareness leads to healing. God was showing me the truth—layer by layer, bit by bit—lovingly and precisely timed. He was showing me that I had value and worth and that it did not depend on any human being.

My father-in-law wanted to tag along with Cate on one of her visits to see Leigh. She re-iterated that he couldn't come, not unless he apologized. Willie didn't miss a beat in protesting. Of course, he wasn't going to apologize because he believed he had nothing to apologize for. So, that was that. Cate asked Leigh whether he wanted to see his father again, and again, Leigh said no.

We were heading into another Christmas, trying to carry on as normal. Brienne was in her final year of college and I had work, but there was nothing normal about it. Now I fully understood how this time of year could be such a paradox, inciting both joy and sorrow. Leigh was in bed all the time now, and we just watched television together if he was awake or I just sat there for a while if he was asleep. At times he felt ice cold, and I would run to the desk for a warmed-up blanket. Then one Saturday morning, as I was shopping for groceries, my cell phone rang. A nurse at the Hen House was telling me that the time was close because Leigh was only semi-conscious.

It is a blur to me now. Who was there at what time? People in and out. The only thing that was on my mind was Leigh, and I was anxious and afraid. At various times throughout the day, Scott and Kristine were there, as well as Erik. Mike spent some time as well.

Brienne and I kept vigil, talking to whoever visited, often glancing at Leigh, but he seemed to be in some transitory state of being—here but not able to respond.

I didn't feel like eating or drinking anything; it was getting late and everyone had gone. I was exhausted, so I proposed to Brienne that we take turns going home for some sleep. Since she was a night owl, I said that I would go first and come back to relieve her in a couple of hours. I went home and managed to relax enough to be half-asleep when my cell phone rang at around two in the morning. Brienne said that Leigh had awakened in great pain, and when she asked the nurse to give him pain medication, the nurse said it wasn't time for his scheduled dose. Apparently, she told my daughter not to worry, that they were taking care of her father, but she refused to give him the medication. I got up, got dressed and went back to the home. Before I reached the room, I ran into the nurse and asked her to give my husband some morphine; she agreed, giving me no trouble.

I was puzzled as to why the nurse gave my daughter a difficult time. She was a twenty-year-old woman now, so it couldn't be because she was a minor. Brienne was annoyed at how she had been dismissed, and I said maybe it was because they could only take the directive from me as Leigh's spouse. As we talked, I noticed that Leigh was nodding his head in agreement. He wasn't out of it the way he had been the entire day. I suggested that Brienne go home for some rest, and Leigh nodded in agreement. She went to the bedside. Leigh took her hand and gently kissed it. I was fighting back my own tears as Brienne told her Dad that she loved him. Leigh couldn't say those words, so he spoke the only phrase he had, "Thank you." After Brienne left, there was silence except for Leigh's breathing, which was more laboured. He was fidgeting, and I was doing anything I could think of to help him get settled. I was gently rubbed his leg, clamping down on my own anxiety because I could feel his. I clasped my hands together in prayer, whispering over and over "Jesus, take him in peace, take him in peace, take him in peace." Leigh's eyes had been closed, but when he heard me, he turned his head and looked right at me, and made a sound as if to say "What?" I said, "I'm praying," and I was astounded as he gave me a slight nod of acknowledgement, then turned his head back. The nurse came in, injected the morphine and left.

Soon after, Leigh's breathing seemed to stop. Then he took a final breath, and it was done. I had never seen or experienced anyone dying in front of me. Knowing it was going to happen didn't lessen the impact. His skin already had a bluish colour, and I was crying as I touched his cheek and told him that I loved him.

Leigh was finally free from the prison he had been in for so long. And, not only that, God wanted him. It was a miracle that he survived, that he had progressed as much as he did with how broken he was. But, I finally understood. God had a master plan and Leigh was the key player. It is written that unless you change and become like a little child, in humility and simplicity, you will not enter the kingdom of heaven. The tragedy transformed Leigh from an angry, prideful man into a gentle, grateful and humble man with a child-like innocence. I know, without a doubt, that Leigh is in a place far better than what anyone could imagine—a place that has to be believed to be seen. The nod that Leigh gave me as I prayed gave me the assurance of his belief. I had often confided in Brienne that if her father had a successful transplant and none of this had happened, I was certain the two of us would not have stayed married.

God took this horrible event and turned it into a testament to His power to transform and redeem. God knew that the lies I believed about my unworthiness were buried deep, so he reached into dark places. He showed me how much I was loved by allowing me to be part of the way and the witness to miracles. Finally, I knew in my soul that I wasn't to blame for someone else's hate or inability to love me, that I never had to prove I was worth being loved. At the same time, He had taken a man who had professed to be an atheist, who had lost almost everything and who had only a handful of words and used him to demonstrate incredible courage and the power of love to overcome. After a lifetime of denial, Leigh was the one to bring the truth out into the light, allowing reconciliation between us and freeing others from deception and manipulation.

I stumbled at times with what God put in front of me. But, in the end, no weapon formed against me prospered. God knew my shortcomings, and more importantly, He knew my heart and He poured out his grace by rendering evil powerless and giving love the final say.

Thank you for reading. If you liked the book, please consider leaving an honest review online where you purchased.

www.ingramcontent.com/pod-product-compliance
Lightning Source LLC
Chambersburg PA
CBHW021327060726

47591CB00006B/1914